Though plays seem to things from c tent throughout is his specified purpose: the examination of moral choice. "The story of a play," he explains, "must be a conflict, and specifically, a conflict between the forces of good and evil within a single person."

Like his fellow modern artists, Anderson sought to define the good, the right, the decent in an increasingly incoherent and indecent world. In terms of form, however, he parted company with the moderns; he trusted classic structures to subdue and organize the chaos of the twentieth century.

Addressing questions of Anderson's artistic and political context, his dramatic theory and form, audience reception here and abroad, these essays open the discourse again on a significant and problematic figure in American theatre.

Maxwell Anderson
and
the New York Stage

Helen Hayes
First Lady of the American theater

Maxwell Anderson

and the New York Stage

Edited by
Nancy J. Doran Hazelton
and
Kenneth Krauss

Library Research Associates Inc.
Monroe, New York
1991

Photos in "The Critical Reception" are courtesy of Städtische Bühnen Münster.

Library Research Associates, Inc.
Dunderberg Road RD#5, Box 41
Monroe, New York 10950

Library of Congress Cataloging-in-Publication Data:

Maxwell Anderson and the New York stage / edited by Nancy J. Doran Hazelton and Kenneth Drauss.
     p.   cm.
Includes bibliographical references and index.
ISBN: 0912526-51-3: $29.95
     1. Anderson, Maxwell, 1888-1959—Stage history—New York (N.Y.)
2. Theater—New York (N.Y.)—History—20th century. I. Hazelton,
Nancy J. Doran, 1948- . II. Krauss, Kenneth, 1948- .
PS3501, NZ56Z76 1991   90-20680
812' .52—dc20   CIP

Acknowledgement

The editors wish to express their profound gratitude and appreciation to the Maxwell Anderson Centennial Committee, Martin F. Schwartz, Director, and to Rockland Community College / SUNY, Suffern, New York, F. Thomas Clark, President.

*Maxwell
Anderson
Centennial
Celebration
1888-1988*

Table of Contents

Preface

This book represents the culmination of a series of events that began on June 13, 1988 with a performance of the late Maxwell Anderson's *Lost in the Stars* and a reception in his honor. It continued with a Lincoln Center exhibition, a film festival, a centennial poster, college and high school activities, a musical retrospective, a video production and a tribute by the Librarian of Congress.

Actually, the Centennial Celebration began in 1986 at a chance meeting between the undersigned and Miss Helen Hayes. Having been a theater buff all my life, I mentioned to Miss Hayes that I remembered vividly her great performance in Maxwell Anderson's *Mary of Scotland* in 1933, and that I was aware of the fact that 1988 would be his centennial year. Her response was, "We ought to do something about it. Max was a dear, dear friend."

Little did she realize that she had planted a seed which was to grow into a veritable garden of festivities.

At the direction of President F. Thomas Clark, Rockland Community College became the sponsor of the Maxwell Anderson Centennial Celebration with Miss Hayes as Chairperson. The other person whose participation was essential was Alan Anderson, Maxwell's son. Alan recalls our first conversation:

> I picked up the phone and after the first identification phrases, was somewhat taken aback when Martin said, "Did you know that your father would have been 100 years old in 1988?" I admitted that I did know, and he followed up with, "What are you doing about it?" Thoroughly cowed, I admitted that nothing had been planned. I thereupon was overwhelmed with Martin's elaborate schemes. For the next two years, I found myself thoroughly involved.

1

Many other people accepted responsibilities; most important was Professor Nancy Hazelton who organized the seminar which became the basis for this book.

The outstanding scholars who responded to our call for papers are an indication of the wisdom of sponsoring the seminar. This volume of new material about an outstanding literary figure of the twentieth century enriches the literature of American drama.

Martin F. Schwartz, Director
Maxwell Anderson Centennial Celebration

Introduction:

Maxwell Anderson and the New York Stage

In *The Quintessence of Ibsenism,* George Bernard Shaw holds the mirror up to Shaw in his tribute to and analysis of Henrik Ibsen. A critic of similar stripe, Maxwell Anderson reveals much about his own art in his 1947 reassessment of Shaw, entitled *St. Bernard.* In this essay, Anderson recants his conviction of 1918 that "Shaw was a brilliant writer but no playwright" (12) and places him rather "at the head of all modern playwrights" (13). This is not to suggest that Anderson was thinking wishfully that the crown would pass to him—though in his glory days some indeed urged it upon him—but like Shaw, he esteems in his predecessor playwright those qualities he recognizes as his own. Of Shaw, Anderson says that

> he has been honest. He has tried hard for absolutes. He has
> tried not to deceive himself or anyone else. And it follows
> that one by one he has taken up and defended, and one by
> one he has abandoned and destroyed, practically "...every
> position a man can take in seeking a faith for himself and
> for mankind." (16)

Maxwell Anderson's search for a faith led him a merry chase as well, and his plays say quite different things from each other. Consistent throughout, however, are the questions raised; Anderson's specified purpose is the examination of moral choice. "The story of a play," he explains in his essay *Off Broadway* (1942), "must be a conflict, and specifically, a conflict between the forces of good and evil within a single person." (25) The forces of evil manifested themselves in all manner of guises during Anderson's long career, and he responded to some of them in plays bound to their time. When the art transcended the politics—as it did, for example, in *Winterset, High Tor,* and *Lost in the Stars*—Anderson seemed to recognize the futility of trying "hard for absolutes," and sought a more human faith. In these plays, Anderson takes his place among the best of modern American playwrights.

3

Born in 1888, Maxwell Anderson witnessed and responded to the tumult of the first half of the twentieth century in America, a time in which—especially after the first World War—new definitions were needed for the good and the beautiful. He was educated at the University of North Dakota and at Stanford; a succession thereafter of teaching and journalistic jobs on both coasts enabled him to support his young family while he made himself ready for his lifework. Only after the commercial success of *What Price Glory* (with Laurence Stallings) in 1924 did he consider himself wholly and truly a playwright; Anderson then abandoned his other endeavors and spent the rest of his life writing primarily for the New York stage.

During his most prolific years, Anderson lived not far from Broadway—across the Hudson River in Rockland County, New York, a decided rural and fairly remote area in those pre-bridge days. This retreat hardly meant disengagement, however, as Anderson produced from here plays that commented upon corruption governmental, judicial, and military, both present and historical.

Like his fellow modern artists, he sought to define the good, the right, the decent in an increasingly incoherent and indecent world, and his stance was appropriately ironic. But in terms of form, he parted company with the moderns: Anderson trusted classic structures; he believed that the chaos of the twentieth century could be organized, even subdued, by the imposition of venerable forms. That he was derivative—a charge laid upon him by detractors—he would surely have acknowledged; Anderson avowed his debt to Aristotle, to Shakespeare, to Keats. It is fair to say, however, that he did something quite new with the structures he pilfered, and he set about deliberately, as he said, to "establish a new convention":

> *Winterset* is largely in verse, but treats a contemporary tragic theme, which makes it more of an experiment that I could wish, for the great masters themselves never tried to make tragic poetry out of the stuff of their own times. ("Poetry" 54)

A century after his birth and 30 years after his death, Anderson's place in the canon has yet to be fixed. Though apart from his time—often in form, sometimes in content—he nonetheless found a popular audience and critical approbation: in the 1930s, he won the Pulitzer Prize and the Drama Critics Circle Award twice. The 40s and 50s were for Anderson productive, though less acclaimed, decades; after his death, however, the answers that he had found in his search—or perhaps the way he chose to present them—were generally regarded as "old-fashioned," and he fell from favor, in terms of both production revivals and dramatic scholarship. No longer current was Anderson's native trust in the efficacy of the spoken word; American theatre language in the 60s and 70s became increasingly colloquial and banal, as the

4

burden of meaning was often carried by gesture and silence. In recent years, however, Anderson's essays into "the upper air of poetic tragedy" ("Poetry" 48) are being considered anew, as the last decades of the century return to their ancient faith in language.

Maxwell Anderson himself recognized that his world was one "in which there are no final answers, in which every life, every nation, and every work of art must be judged and rejudged in successive years or generations as long as its influence endures" ("Thoughts" 3). It is fitting that now, during the Maxwell Anderson Centennial Celebration year, and here, in Rockland County, New York, that we look again at the nature and quality of Anderson's search and attempt to rejudge its success.

This volume of essays provides no final answers on Maxwell Anderson; indeed several contributors pose new questions that point to the need for further Anderson research, particularly vis-a-vis the playwright's audience. The collection does, however, open discussion again on a significant figure in American theatre history whose corpus remains problematic for those who could fit him in and more so, given his achievements, for those who would leave him out.

Anderson's historic context is examined by two contributors. Beverle Bloch looks at the New York theatrical season of 1924-25, one which four new American plays met with success—Anderson and Stallings' *What Price Glory*, O'Neill's *Desire Under the Elms*, Howard's *They Knew What They Wanted,* and Lawson's *Processional*—and argues that the critical and popular approbation these very different plays met with betokens a moving away from European dominance, a "coming of age" for American drama. In his essay, Harold Cantor focuses on the following decades, on Anderson's involvement with the Group Theater and his tempestuous relationship with Clifford Odets. Anderson and Odets, according to Cantor, "shared a similar problem: how to break out of the narrow mold of naturalism...and to embody the American themes Clurman had urged on both of them in the heightened language of poetry." Although they disagreed finally on the nature and the proper treatment of "American themes," both playwrights found a poetic form appropriate to the matter they explored.

Placing Anderson in the wider context of nineteenth and twentieth-century political thought and political drama, Thomas P. Adler finds the playwright's 1933 *Both Your Houses* informed with the fundamental distrust of majority rule articulated by Alexis de Tocqueville, John Stuart Mill, and Henry Adams, and dramatized by Ibsen in *An Enemy of the People*. Adler traces the messianic political drama, a form supported by "the idealistic belief held by authors such as Thoreau that character and intellect could make a difference," through the 40s and 50s, but identifies in the 60s a shift away from "the side of possibility" to satire and despair in political drama, which he contends persists in contemporary American theatre.

Perry D. Luckett and Randall J. Buchanan address the making of Anderson's plays. Comparing the dramatic "rules" Anderson presented in his theoretical essays with his work for the theatre, Buchanan argues correspondence between the playwright's adherence to the prescriptions of his "Poetics" and the commercial success of particular plays. Luckett as well searches the theoretical pronouncements of Anderson, on both poetry and drama, in an attempt to reconcile the contrary views of his moral philosophy held by Anderson critics. Acknowledging that Anderson seemed during some periods the idealist and some the pessimist, Luckett argues that Anderson's "vision was never static," and that only an assessment of his whole career reveals the skepticism and the uncertainty from which his plays issue.

Anderson's collaborations with Kurt Weill provide the subject for John Bush Jones in his essay on Anderson as a lyricist. In reviewing the function of song in both *Knickerbocker Holiday* (1938) and *Lost in the Stars* (1940), Jones finds neither play conforming to the conventions of American musical theatre of that time: "the former in many ways harks back to…the comic operas of Gilbert and Sullivan, while the latter is a somewhat daring, forward-looking, even experimental piece adumbrating later innovations in musical theatre form and style."

Ron Engle presents a comprehensive and invaluable research document detailing foreign language productions of Anderson's plays seen on European stages. "The production history," Engle has discovered, "begins in Berlin with the 1929 Piscator production of *Rivalen (What Price Glory)* and ends with the Städtische Bühnen Münster production of *Knickerbocker Holiday* produced as West Germany's celebration of Anderson's 100th birthday." Translated productions have been mounted as well in Czechoslovakia, Finland, France, Greece, Italy, Latvia, Lithuania, Norway, Poland, Sweden, and Switzerland; Engle registers production specifics for each in his appendix.

The final documents locate Maxwell Anderson in the present. In his interview with George Schaefer, Arthur B. Friedman queries him on a UCLA production of *Winterset* that both were currently involved with—Schaefer as director, Friedman as actor. William R. Klink's annotated bibliography updates his earlier *Maxwell Anderson and S.N. Behrman: A Reference Guide*; the listings here draw from work published between 1980 and 1988. The coda to this collection, "Maxwell Who?" is provided by the playwright's son Alan Anderson.

Nancy J. Doran Hazelton
Rockland Community College/SUNY

Kenneth Krauss
The College of Saint Rose

6

Works Cited

Anderson, Maxwell. "Off Broadway." *Off Broadway: Essays about the Theater*. New York: Sloan, 18-35.

___. "Poetry in the Theatre." *Off Broadway: Essays about the Theater*. New York: Sloan, 47-54.

___. "St. Bernard." *Off Broadway: Essays about the Theater*. New York: Sloan, 12-17.

___. "Thoughts about the Critics." *Off Broadway: Essays about the Theater*. New York: Sloan, 3-11.

American Drama Comes of Age

on the New York Stage: 1924-25

by Beverle Bloch
Bowling Green State University

As students of the American theatre know, there was relatively little interest in serious drama in the United States until the second decade of the twentieth century. Until that time, commercial interests prevailed and the professional American theatre produced a steady diet of melodrama and other forms of light entertainment. However, as early as 1912, small groups of young artists and intellectuals began meeting in New York's Greenwich Village to discuss European art movements. Many young Americans went abroad to study and observe. Foreign touring companies such as the Abbey Theatre and the Ballets Russes stirred additional interest. The intellectual and artistic activity culminated in the formation of a number of *art* theatres, that is, theatres that put artistic concerns above commercial concerns. Two seminal art theatres, the Washington Square Players and the Provincetown Players, both opened their doors in New York City in the year 1915. The efforts of these two groups in combination with a few maverick commercial producers would be responsible for changing the direction of modern American drama and theatre.

Like many art theatres of the period, the Washington Square Players and the Provincetown Players shared a desire to experiment with innovations in drama and staging that had surfaced in Europe toward the end of the nineteenth century. However, these two fledgling companies had another goal on their agenda. Both groups evinced an interest in producing the works of untried American dramatists. In this regard, the two companies differed slightly: The Provincetown Players produced only native, original works, while the Washington Square Players balanced their productions with contemporary works of European authorship. In their formative years, however, the two groups produced a combined total of 131 original American dramas (Durham 380 and Eaton 29).

9

Although both the Washington Square and the Provincetown Players began as amateur theatre groups, both had reorganized and become professional by the early twenties. For the Washington Square Players, the end came when too many of its members left to join the war effort, in 1918. A short time later, however, several past members regrouped to form the Theatre Guild. Firmly rooted in the experiences of the Washington Square Players, the newly-formed Guild was to some degree an extension of this group. Much like its predecessor, the Guild expressed a desire to produce "plays of artistic merit not ordinarily produced by the commercial managers" (Langner 118). However, in contrast to the Players, the Guild did not plan to give preference to scripts by American authors. Instead, the new producing entity concentrated on presenting works by European playwrights for reasons outlined by Guild Board Director Lawrence Langner:

> During the first few years of the Theatre Guild's career, there were no playwrights in America of the stature of Chekhov, Shaw, and Galsworthy, with the exception of Eugene O'-Neill who was connected with the Provincetown Players. It was my feeling...that we should produce the important plays of European authors to set a standard for American writers. (Langner 142)

In keeping with this policy, the Guild produced only three plays of American authorship during its first five seasons.

Although the Provincetown Playhouse managed to hang onto its amateur status slightly longer than the Washington Square Players, by the early twenties it too was in the throes of reorganization. In 1923, when the reorganized Provincetown Playhouse opened its doors, it was under the control of what is generally referred to as the triumvirate—the combined leadership of Kenneth Macgowan, Eugene O'Neill and designer Robert Edmond Jones. This change led to the development of a professional experimental theatre company dedicated to producing experimental drama, both American and foreign.

One additional source of exciting and innovative theatre during this period was the maverick commercial producer, Arthur Hopkins. After brief stints in journalism and the business end of vaudeville, Hopkins went abroad to observe new developments in European theatre. When he returned, he undertook a number of unique productions, including an expressionist-style *Macbeth*, designed by Robert Edmond Jones, that created a sensation with its use of huge witches' masks suspended above the stage (Brockett 496). Although primarily associated with the classics and works by modern European authors, Hopkins had also demonstrated an interest in American drama. In 1914 he co-produced Elmer Rice's *On Trial*, and in 1921 he produced O'Neill's *Anna Christie*.

New directions in theatre to some degree echoed the turbulence of the time. It was a decade of change. Uprooted by the war, Americans were breaking with the past and moving from one part of the country to another—principally into cities where they became social emigres. In the cities, they clashed with the legions who had migrated to these centers at the end of the nineteenth century. Migration continued a process begun during World War I. For the first time in history millions of Americans were being brought into contact with different people and different ideas. Moreover, social mores and roles were changing, especially the roles of women. It was the day of the flapper—the girl with the bobbed hair and short skirts. The radical change in fashion was associated with a new attitude toward sex. By the twenties, Freud's theories had become widely known, providing a new word to describe all the world's ills: repression. Through a misunderstanding of his theories, many assumed that Freud was arguing that "unless you freely expressed your libido and gave outlet to your sex energy, you would damage your health" (Leuchtenburg 159). Other social roles were in flux as Prohibition caused many Americans to become lawbreakers and criminals. Another segment of the population, the young, were alienated from the establishment because of their experiences with World War I. The war had been won, but many of the returned soldiers had bitter feelings about the generation in control of national life. Still other Americans, perhaps in reaction to this growing spirit of change and liberality, voted for mediocrity—or "normalcy"—in electing President Warren Harding, while Congress rejected the League of Nations. The nation also witnessed one of the most hysterical witch-hunts in modern history in a frenzied response to the Bolshevik revolution in Russia, when United States Attorney General A. Mitchell Palmer had thousands of Americans thrown into jail on suspicion of collaborating with the Russians (Atkinson 196-8).

In the midst of this upheaval, Broadway, both as an art form and as a source of entertainment, was booming, climbing toward a peak of popularity that would never be repeated. New theatres were quickly being built as producers scrambled to produce plays that would appeal to its rapidly growing audience. Changes in volume of production corresponded to changes in the nature and function of theatre. For theatre historian John Gassner, the "push" of this period forced Broadway to set standards which "stamped modernity upon our theatre" (vii). Oliver M. Sayler, writing in 1923, described the American theatre as going through a "period of wakening" (1), while James O'Donnell Bennett, writing for *The Drama* noted, "Most of us date back to the time when the stage was the nation's entertainment. We have come into a time when it is more and more valiantly becoming the nation's heart-searcher and mind-disturber" (27).

At first, changes in theatre practice were based on developments that had already taken place in Europe. Many of the plays produced by the Theatre Guild and other groups were written by European playwrights. However, by the mid-twenties, theatregoers were becoming weary of European dominance in the theatre. They began expressing an interest in drama that would serve as an interpreter of domestic concerns. The spirit of the times bore fruit during the New York theatre season of 1924-25, with the success of *What Price Glory* by Lawrence Stallings and Maxwell Anderson, *Desire Under the Elms* by Eugene O'Neill, *They Knew What They Wanted* by Sidney Howard, and the experimental "jazz-drama" *Processional* by theatrical and political rebel John Howard Lawson. It was the first time that the "new" American drama merited more than token representation on the New York stage. All four plays were well received by critics, and all four were financially successful as well (Rathburn). As a result, it can be argued that it was in this season that American drama "came of age." In this paper, I shall examine these four plays, noting how each attempted to solve the problem of creating a new kind of American drama.

What Price Glory opened at the Plymouth Theatre on September 5, 1924. Produced by Arthur Hopkins, the play purported to tell the story of war "as it has not been presented theatrically for thousands of years" (Hinkley 4). In contrast to traditional war plays of the period which were based on appeals to patriotism and sentiment, the Anderson-Stallings play gave a pragmatic, non-idealized depiction of the culture associated with war. The play's most notable asset was its use of language—"as fine and free a use of American language as our theatre has known" (Hinkley 4). *What Price Glory* is primarily a play of character and language; plot is of secondary importance. The play's most notable character is Captain Flagg, a career soldier, cynical, competent, and drunk whenever the opportunity arises. A description is provided by his nemesis Sergeant Quirt:

> You ought to seen him in China. Straight as a mast, muscled
> like a gorilla. Christian as hell. Good deal of liquor has
> flowed under his belt since then. (Gassner 67)

Perhaps he is best described in his own words, spoken to two lieutenants direct from headquarters who, according to the stage directions, are "…just like tailor's dummies of a Burberry outfit slicked to the notch and perky and eager" (Gassner 79). Flagg welcomes them with these words:

> My name is Flagg, gentlemen, and I'm the sinkhole and
> cesspool of this regiment, frowned on in the Y.M.C.A. huts
> and sneered at by the divisional Beau Brummells. I am a
> lousy, good-for-nothing company commander. I corrupt
> youth and lead little boys astray into the black shadows
> between the lines of hell, killing more men that any other
> company commander in the regiment, and drawing all the
> dirty jobs in the world. I take chocolate soldiers and make
> dead heroes out of them. (Gassner 80)

Flagg cares about his men although he is gruff to their faces. A telling scene occurs when "little" Lewisohn wants to report a lost identification tag. Flagg tells him,

> Well, I thought I'd been around a good deal, and I've had 'em ask me to show 'em where they live and button up their pants for them and put on their little night-drawers, but I'm a son-of-a-gun if this isn't the first time anybody has ever asked me to help him find his identification tag! (Gassner 62)

Flagg makes light of the loss, saying to Lewisohn, "If you want to know what your name is look in your hat," but then he tells a corporal to "get him a new tag if they have to build a new factory in Hoboken to turn it out," because he knows that the kid is "dying of grief away from his mother" (Gassner 62).

The plot of *What Price Glory* concerns a triangle between Flagg, Charmaine, and the new first Sergeant, Quirt, described by one character as a "a top with two glass eyes, a slit across his face for a mouth and a piece out of his ear" (Gassner 61). Charmaine, the inn-keeper's daughter, is a camp follower. She loves the Captain, but if he goes away she will love someone else. When the play begins, the Captain is about to go to Paris, leaving the new Sergeant in charge. There is bad blood between the two, and Quirt seizes the opportunity to make love to the Captain's girl. When the Captain finds out, and also learns that Charmaine's father is preparing to lay charges, he tries to force Quirt to marry her. At the end of the act, his plot falls through as the war beckons and Flagg tells Charmaine: "I'm damn sorry I have to take your sergeant away...It's a hell of a war but it's the only one we've got" (Gassner 74).

Charmaine is a major character, but she is not developed. She functions as a pawn in the "war" between Quirt and Flagg, the relationship that is at the heart of the play. At times they function as colleagues, at times they try to kill each other, and both activities are part of the game. In the second act Quirt is wounded. This means he can return to Charmaine. He's already shown that he doesn't really care about her, but he seizes on the opportunity to get one up on the Captain. Through a complicated series of events, the Captain gets a lead and the two men return to town within minutes of each other. They play blackjack, and the Captain wins, but before he can take advantage of his situation, he learns that his leave has been cancelled and that he must return to the front. Quirt is left with the girl, but he too decides to leave her even though he can legitimately stay behind because he is wounded. His last line, and the last line of the play, is "What a lot of God damn fools it takes to make a war! Hey, Flagg, wait for baby!" (Gassner 89).

The most controversial speech in the play comes during the face- off between Quirk and Flagg in the last act when Charmaine implores the men not to fight. Flagg replies,

> The hell you say! First time in six months I've had a good reason for fighting. The Germans don't want my woman. I been fighting them for eight dollars a day. (Gassner 87)

This scene was troubling to patriots and those who wanted to espouse patriotic sentiments. An example of this point of view can be seen in a review of the play by the conservative reviewer, Arthur Hornblow, who argued that the play was not a faithful picture of war:

> [We] are shown only the sordidness, the stark horror, the filth and bestiality of war and its reactions on the men dragged from office desks and comfortable homes to suffer all its misery. The play shows only that side. The other side of the picture—the spiritual exaltation of the young warrior as he responds to his country's call, buckling on his armor to defend home and loved ones, the individual deeds of heroism, the self-sacrifice of the badly wounded soldier emptying his water flask to slake the thirst of a dying comrade, the noble work of mercy done by the women nurses—all that is conveniently ignored. Apparently, for the purpose of making the picture as repellent as possible, only the meanest types are shown, men moved by the worst passions and most ignoble instincts. (15)

Hornblow's review is an excellent example of the idealist view of war popular in the nineteenth century.

As would happen to many of the plays during this period, *What Price Glory* aroused the ire of the authorities. Objections came both from the military and from local authorities, but no legal remedies were necessary. The objections of the military never became formal charges while producer Hopkins removed "three strong expressions" to keep the civil authorities from arresting the cast ("History" 14). The censorship controversy lent special emphasis to a note from Theodore Roosevelt which read in part:

> "As I see it, this play does not teach that vice is commendable, but that a man may have vices and yet be heroic. If it is bad to show that a man can have vices and yet the major virtues—then this play is bad. If it is good to show that rough and dissipated as man may be in many ways, they yet can

be brave and do fine deeds—then this play is good. I hold
that it is good". ("History" 13).

Roosevelt's point of view was shared by the majority of the theatregoing public who boosted the play to "hit" status (Rathburn). Easily the most popular of the four plays under discussion, its success led one reviewer to assert, "No American play by an American dramatist has won such sharp success or satisfied so wide a circle of critics and playgoers as *What Price Glory"* (Dickenson 723).

Designed by Woodman Thomson, *What Price Glory* featured a box set in keeping with the realist style prevalent at that time. Noting that the sets were "fair but without a creative and dramatic relationship to the play," Stark Young added, "'What Price Glory' is not one of those examples of the art of the theatre that discover a story, a pattern of action that is in itself the very essence and expression of the play" (4).

Though its staging was undistinguished, the play made its mark on American theatre through its use of language and its depiction of war. For Burns Mantle, the play marks an epoch in New York play producing history because

> in addition to performing the great service of debunking the essentially untrue and no more than prettily patriotic war play, it served to crystallize a growing rebellion of young moderns who were protesting the conventional limitations of artificial stage dialogue. It tore down old puritan barriers that had for many generations stood as a protection against the use of any and all profanity on the stage. It established the license if not the rights of soldiers in stage trenches to talk as much like soldiers in real trenches as a liberal interpretation of what constitutes decency and good taste would permit. ("Contemporary" 42-3)

Noting that *What Price Glory* was the most outspoken play of its time, John Gassner credits the play with doing more than any other play to promote the cause of realism and freedom of speech on the American stage (Gassner 58).

Desire Under the Elms opened on Tuesday, November 11, 1924, at the Greenwich Village Theatre, a second venue leased by the Provincetown Players to house large-scale efforts or productions which promised popular success. Set in New England, *Desire Under the Elms* is based on a reworking of the myths surrounding two Greek heroines—Phaedra and Medea. Although the play can be considered an example of realism, O'Neill continued his practice of working with his own symbols. The play takes its title from the setting, described in the stage directions as the exterior of a farmhouse flanked by huge elms that

> bend their trailing branches down over the roof. They appear to protect and at the same time subdue. There is a sinister maternity in their aspect, a crushing, jealous absorption. They have developed from their intimate contact with the life of man in the house an appalling humaneness. They brood oppressively over the house. They are like exhausted women resting their sagging breasts and hands and hair on its roof, and when it rains their tears trickle down monotonously and rot on the shingles. (Gassner 28)

The major characters in *Desire Under the Elms* are Ephraim Cabot, a hard and self-righteous patriarch; Eben, a son by his second wife; and Abbie Putnam, a young woman who has married Ephraim in his old age because she wants a home. To further her claim, Abbie sleeps with Eben, hoping to become pregnant with an heir. Her plan succeeds, but in the process, she falls in love with Eben and gives up her desire to keep him from inheriting the farm. Through a misunderstanding, Eben loses his faith in Abbie and forswears his love for her. To prove her loyalty, Abbie kills the child. As the play ends, the two enjoy a brief reconciliation, but both are taken away by the sheriff to answer for the murder. Like Strindberg before him, O'Neill dramatizes the battle of the sexes. The symbolic oppression of the "female" elms is juxtaposed with Ephraim's hard-hearted maleness, and the hardness of the stony rocks that make up the soil of the farm. When Ephraim learns that his heir has been murdered, he replies, "I am hard. I am a hard man and I am alone—but so is God." O'Neill's characters, like Ibsen's Brand, do not settle for half.

As a result, *Desire Under the Elms* verges on the tragic. According to Joseph Wood Krutch, *Desire Under the Elms* shows O'Neill experimenting with ways to dramatize passion:

> As a young man, O'Neill first equated passion with wild and uncontrolled circumstances such as the sea...the mature O'Neill has learned that where there is most smoke there is not necessarily most fire. He has learned that souls confined...by very virtue of the fact that they have no outlet explode finally with the greatest spiritual violence. (Krutch, "Stumps" 578)

Of all the plays discussed in this paper, *Desire Under the Elms* is the best known. Arguably O'Neill's first major play, it continues to be read, discussed, and staged. A complete critical history of this play is beyond the scope of this article. Rather, I will concentrate on a comparison between this play and the others in terms of developments in the emerging American theatre. Seen from this perspective, the play is of interest because of its innovative staging. Designed by Robert Edmond Jones, the play's well-known set featured four windows, through which the characters could be viewed as they moved through the house. The innovative set allowed for numerous juxtapositions that provided a visual representation of the play's complicated relationships. An excellent example is the scene preceding Abbie's seduction of Eben. Ephraim and Abbie are in their bedroom, and Ephraim is telling Abbie his life story. He attempts to make contact with Abbie in his long monologues, but it is clear that Abbie is ignoring him while she tries to figure out what Eben is doing on the other side of the wall. At the same time we see Eben seemingly staring at Abbie through the wall. The flexible set reinforces the growing relationship between Abbie and Eben at Ephraim's expense.

O'Neill made sketches of the unit set and gave them to Jones before Jones made his designs. As a result, O'Neill was upset when the set became known as "Bobbie's house" (Wainscott 161). The fact that O'Neill conceived of the play with the set in mind helps to explain its truly organic relationship to the text. In its original production, then, *Desire Under the Elms* may be considered a landmark in American scene design because it featured a set that was an integral component of the play.

Desire Under the Elms was well acted and well produced, but despite the serious nature of this play, it succeeded largely due to its "titter factor." Krutch notes,

> Many saw it either to giggle at the scene in which Eben is seduced or to raise righteous hands in indignation that such obscenity should be permitted. Still others, fashionable intellectuals, took it as an attack upon puritanism, a bold muchraking expose of what really went on in the prim houses of our revered forebears. (Krutch, *American* 96-7)

Banned in Boston, the play continued to arouse controversy when it toured the conservative midwest. Some reviewers found O'Neill's negativity unpatriotic. Sample headlines reveal some of the sentiment aroused by the play: "New O'Neill Play Sinks to Depths"; "Naked Nastiness of Horrible Plot, Entirely Morbid, Cheap, Uninteresting and Utterly Disagreeable"; and "O'-Neill Still Full of Gloom: Playwright Reveals Revolting Story of Life on New England Farm." From W. C. Robertson of the *Minneapolis Star* came this epitaph: "As entertainment it registers zero...as a stab in the back to the so-called legitimate stage...[the] play should be sprinkled generously with ashes and then shoveled into the sewer."

Produced by the Theatre Guild, Sidney Howard's *They Knew What They Wanted* opened on November 24 at the Guild's Garrick Theatre. Set in the Napa Valley, the play featured an in-depth look at Italian-American wine-growers. Like *What Price Glory* and *Desire Under the Elms, They Knew What They Wanted* is based on a love triangle. The main characters are Tony, a sixty year-old Italian immigrant who owns a vineyard in the Napa Valley; Joe, an I.W.W. organizer who has been working for Tony as a hired hand; and Amy, a former waitress in a San Francisco spaghetti joint who needs a home.

Tony sees Amy in the spaghetti joint and falls in love with her. Too shy to introduce himself, he returns home and proposes marriage to her by mail. Unknown to Joe, he sends Joe's picture to Amy instead of his own. Amy agrees to the marriage, and the play begins on her wedding day, the day she is supposed to arrive in the Napa Valley and marry Tony. Through a series of unlucky breaks, Tony has an accident in his car and fails to meet his bride-to-be at the train station. When Amy arrives at Tony's home, she meets Joe first, and thinks he is the groom. She doesn't figure out the truth until Tony, unconscious with a broken leg, is carried into the house. Her first response, "Who is that old guy?" is followed by the rude understanding that the "old guy" is the man she's agreed to marry. Furious because of the deception, she initially vents her anger on Joe. When she calms down, she decides to stay and make the best of things. The wedding takes place as planned, even though Tony is unable to walk. Later that night, in a fit of loneliness and anger, Amy sleeps with Joe. Time passes, and Amy forgets about the interlude. She begins to like, even love Tony and starts to feel at home. At this point she learns that she is pregnant. Tony, an invalid still, cannot possibly be the father.

Like *What Price Glory, They Knew What They Wanted* is written in a realistic style. It has only one set, a box set which recreates the downstairs and front porch of Tony's home. Unlike *What Price Glory*, however, Howard uses the set to give clues to the play's development. For example, the play begins in summer and ends during the harvest season. According to the stage directions, the outside of the house is covered with vines. When the play begins, Howard stipulates that the vines are "*small and green*"; in the last act, three months later, the vines are "*large and purple*" (Gassner 92). Howard also uses set dressing to define Tony's ethnicity. When the play begins, there are pictures of George Washington and Garibaldi on the walls. Because the house is ready for a wedding, it is decorated. Howard calls for decorations that combine "the red, white and green of Italy with the red, white and blue of these United States," adding, "the picture of Garibaldi is draped with an American flag, the picture of Washington with an Italian flag" (Gassner 92). In the third act, after Amy has become part of the family, changes in decor signal her changed relationship to the house. Now the stage directions describe the addition of "handsome, though inexpensive cretonne curtains" on the windows and new shades on the lamps. In addition, new pictures "selected from the stock-in-trade of almost any provincial 'art department' have replaced Washington and Garibaldi" (Gassner 114).

They Knew What They Wanted is based on two major compromises. The first occurs when Amy decides to stay in the Napa Valley even though it means she has to marry the "old guy." In a dialogue with Joe she quickly runs through her options, exclaiming,

> Oh, God! Oh, my God! I got to go back and wait on table! What'll all those girls say when they see me? And I ain't even got the price of my ticket! (Gassner 103)

Amy has thrown over her old life and spent every cent on a trousseau. Joe tells Amy that Tony will reimburse her, but Amy begins to think. The stage directions note her process of ratiocination:

> AMY picks up the few belongings she has left about the room. She stands a moment holding them, looking about her, at the four walls, at the country outside. Then her eye falls upon JOE's photograph which still lies, face-up, on the table. She takes it in her hand and looks at it. Mechanically she makes as though to put it into the bosom of her dress. She changes her mind, drops it on the table and looks around her again. She seems to reach a decision. Her face sets and she pushes the photograph vigorously away from her.... (Gassner 103)

Her decision made, she tells Joe.

> No I ain't going. Why should I go? I like the country. This place suits me all right. It's just what I was looking for. I'm here and I might as well stick. I guess he ain't so bad, at that. I guess I could have done a lot worse. If he wants to marry me, I'm game. I'm game to see it through. It's nice up here. (Gassner 103)

As she ends her outburst, the stage directions note that Amy "...pulls off her hat and sits, exhausted..." while Joe stares at her "...in mute admiration" (Gassner 103).

The second compromise occurs near the end of the play when Tony learns that Amy is pregnant. At first he reaches for the shot gun, edging toward the Eugene O'Neill world of no forgiveness. He sobs terribly, but then it is his turn to think. A stream of questions burst from his lips. How will Amy manage; who will take care of her? Joe says he'll do the right thing, but Tony will have none of it. He tells Amy,

> I get excite' just now...Excuse! Excuse! I think verra good once more. You ain't goin' with Joe. You stayin' here with Tony just like nothin' is happen', an' by an' by da little fella

is come...What you done was a mistake in da head, not in
da heart...Mistake in da head is no matter. (Gassner 121)

At this, Tony tells Joe to leave, and as the curtain falls we see Tony and Amy
embracing, while the stage directions note "TONY clutches her even closer as
the curtain falls" (Gassner 122).

They Knew What They Wanted dramatizes the art of compromise and
restraint, showing that characters can get what they want, even if those things
don't always come in shiny, new packages. Joe wants his freedom, Amy wants
a home and Tony wants a wife and child, and although none of them come
through the experience unblemished, all three, in the end, do get what they
want. Joe's last line, "I guess there ain't none of us got any kick comin', at
that" (Gassner 122) shows that he too understands this principle.

In many ways, They Knew What They Wanted is comparable to What
Price Glory. Both plays are realistic, both utilize the vernacular, and both stress
pragmatism and compromise. Moreover, both debunk an idealized system of
assigning value, preferring to look reality in the eye. In What Price Glory, it
is patriotism and the glamour of war that get this treatment; in They Knew What
They Wanted, it is marriage and the idealized portrayal of women. In Shavian
terms, both plays move away from idealism toward realism, although neither
playwright strives to prove a thesis. In The American Theatre Since 1918,
Krutch compares these plays to Shakespearian drama, arguing that both
explore the emotional consequences of newly established moral and intellectual convictions (43). Krutch adds that both playwrights assume moral attitudes in their audience that at the time were considered "advanced" (50).
They Knew What They Wanted was extremely successful. It ran 192 performances, toured successfully, and was awarded the Pulitzer Prize. Despite this,
They Knew What They Wanted drew criticism for its use of language and was
often compared to What Price Glory in this regard. New York Tribune reviewer
Percy Hammond wrote that They Knew What They Wanted "abounds in
profanity worse than What Price Glory" while New York Telegraph reviewer
James P. Sinnott claimed that sitting in the audience gave one "the nervous
feeling that the police may break in and drag everyone out in a patrol wagon"
because of the strong language. And in the midwest, Detroit News reporter
George Stark warned his readers, "again it becomes a duty (as in the case of
What Price Glory) to sound a note of caution to those who demand chastity in
theme and language in their dramatic fare."

Many reviewers also noted the similarity in plot and theme between
They Knew What They Wanted and Desire Under the Elms. Both plays are
dramas of encroachment in which a woman who is an outsider wants a home.
In addition, both plays involve a love triangle with an illegitimate heir fathered
by a younger man. In an article written for Theatre Arts Monthly, Edmund
Wilson wrote a tongue-in-cheek version of They Knew What They Wanted as
it might have been written by Eugene O'Neill:

If O'Neill had written this play, the lover would have come back again. This would have demoralized the girl and she would have taken to drink. The old man, seeing that something was wrong would have become morbid about the child and at last, discovering that Amy was still untrue to him, would have strangled it in a fury. Then the girl would have killed herself and the lover would have shot the old man and himself been finally apprehended by the California police for an I.W.W. crime which he had never committed. (78)

Wilson seems to prefer this version, but Howard had another lesson in mind. His play is more hopeful, a wry comedy of human failings rather than a tragedy where an unforgiving God declares that halfway measures are not enough. For Howard, unlike Brand, the art of life is seen to be a combination of tolerance and compromise.

Despite differences, one can find definite similarities in *What Price Glory, Desire Under the Elms,* and *They Knew What They Wanted.* All three plays are examples of a developing American realist style. All feature a use of vernacular, a type of realist staging, and a plot that hinges on the relationship between two men and a woman. If *What Price Glory* and *They Knew What They Wanted* dramatize the emotional problems that accompany shifts in social mores, *Desire Under the Elms* can be seen to dramatize the tragic consequences that accompany a hard-hearted resistance to change. Thus, all three plays have some relationship to the change-ridden society that spawned them. However, in the last play to be discussed, John Howard Lawson's *Processional,* one does not have to search for this connection. In *Processional,* Lawson set out to create a play that would, by virtue of its form, express the rhythm and spirit of its time. Like O'Neill, Lawson had grandiose aims, but they were stated in terms of form rather than theme. Lawson disliked realism and believed that its closed nature did not correspond to the changing times. Thus, Lawson strove to create a distinctly American dramatic form, capable of expressing America in the twenties. In the preface to *Processional,* Lawson explains that he is trying to create a dramatic form capable of reflecting "the color and movement of the American processional as it streams about us" (Lawson ix). Subtitled a "jazz symphony of American Life," *Processional* combined the raucous energy of jazz, vaudeville, and burlesque with a prolabor, anticapitalist critique of American society in which he even included the Ku Klux Klan. Unlike the three other plays under discussion, *Processional* is not a drama of character. Rather, *Processional* is peopled with vaudeville stereotypes, including a Yiddish comic, a Polish anarchist, and a black man named "Rastus." Lawson used these types to make a comment on the ethnic and racial stereotypes that had been prevalent in vaudeville. He also mixed elements of various dramatic styles, using bits of drama, comedy, melodrama, and farce in an attempt to comment on the theatre itself. Most important, according to Lawson, was his rejection of the stage illusion common to both realism and expressionism. Instead he turned to the presentational style of vaudeville, burlesque, and cabaret, experimenting with a kind of theatricalism which makes no attempt to create theatrical illusion.

Processional made its debut on January 13, 1925. Produced by the Theatre Guild, it took over the Garrick Theatre where *They Knew What They Wanted* had been playing. The basic plot of *Processional* concerns a mining strike loosely based on the labor strife in Mingo County, West Virginia, which involved a strike among miners of various ethnic and racial backgrounds. In *Processional,* one of the striking miners, Jim Flimmins, escapes from jail, kills a soldier, rapes a Jewish "jazz baby" named Sadie, and then flees town after being blinded by the Ku Klux Klan. In the final act, the Ku Klux Klan attempts to drive the pregnant Sadie out of town, but Jim returns and marries her. The marriage and impending birth create a kind of spiritual regeneration that reunites the people of the town. The strike is settled and the Ku Klux Klan members return to the fold as loyal workers.

One interesting stylistic innovation in *Processional* was the use of a rag-tag bunch of striking miners, each representing a different ethnic stereotype, who played jazz on make-shift instruments. These "jazz miners" functioned as a kind of Greek Chorus, bridging the gap between actors and audience by entering and exiting into the orchestra pit, thereby breaking the illusion of the fourth wall. (Lawson had wanted entrances and exits through the audience but this was vetoed by the Guild Board.) In addition, Lawson used the characters' dialects to provide a source of rhythm, giving the play a jazzy feel. An example of this is the scene where Sadie first meets the Jazz Miners:

> RASTUS: Wanna join the Coal Town jazz, Kid? Wanna step
> along in the big peerade with us guys?
> SADIE: I'd be scared.
> GORE: Wanna play, kid?
> SADIE: I like this one cause it slides so funny.
> WAYNE: Aw, give it to her…Gentlemen, lemme introduce:
> Miss Sadie Cohen, about to tickle the slide trombone. (Lawson 12)

Another interesting aspect of the play was its staging. In keeping with the vaudeville motif, Lawson called for vaudevillesque staging with no illusion. Scene designer Mordecai Gorelik gave Lawson what he wanted, creating a series of one-dimensional drop curtains in a variety of styles. The opening drop curtain, Main Street on the fourth of July, was particularly effective in setting the tone of the production.

From a contemporary point of view, there is nothing particularly unusual about Lawson's goals and dramaturgy. His desire to work with a popular aesthetic combined with his dislike of realism is reminiscent of some of the theoretical writings of Bertolt Brecht, while his desire to comment on theatrical realism can be compared to Luigi Pirandello's in *Six Characters in Search of an Author* (1921). Lawson's use of vaudevillian conventions foreshadows Samuel Beckett's use of traditions associated with the Irish music hall in *Waiting for Godot* (1952-53). Although *Processional's* experimental technique can be discussed from a contemporary perspective, it was almost completely inexplicable in 1925. Eyewitness reports suggest that when *Processional* opened, its audience was completely mystified. Although many artists, writers and even a few critics hailed *Processional* for its originality and formal experimentation, other critics declared that the work had neither form nor content. Burns Mantle called the work "jumble drama," adding, "It is satire and muttered raving. It is life out of focus like Caligari's dream" ("Processional" 16). From Alan Dale of the *American* came the pronouncement, "The only thing in its favor was that you could come when you pleased, leave when you pleased and miss nothing." *Post* reviewer John Anderson added, "He [Lawson] had nothing to say. Jazz had nothing to say, and both of them said it violently for two hours and a half." Although *Processional* did not tour, newspapers across the country covered the controversy. Many reprinted the New York reviews, sometimes with new, imaginative headlines. The *Cleveland News* reprinted Burns Mantle's review with the heading "Guild Trots Out its Padded Cell Play." The same review in the *Denver Post* bore the heading, "Life Out of Focus is Shown in Latest production That Came from Diseased Brain." When the Guild scheduled an open forum to discuss the play at a New York theatre, thousands showed. Thus, *Processional* soon came to be known as the most discussed play of all time, rivaling the controversy over *What Price Glory, Desire Under the Elms* and *They Knew What The Wanted*. Once again, a serious American play had engendered controversy. *Processional* had other things in common with these three plays. It too, used a type of vernacular speech, focused on ethnic themes, and suggested a new morality. Like *They Knew What They Wanted,* it glorified tolerance and compromise. But *Processional* also contributed some new elements. Its use of themes borrowed from labor and the political arena foreshadowed the social drama of the thirties, while the combination of popular culture and politics suggests a comparison with the work of Brecht and Meyerhold.

Thus, in one season, American dramatists ran the gamut from Ibsen to Brecht, experimenting and perfecting while they mocked, debunked, and undermined. These four plays range from realism to anti-realism, utilizing new stagecraft, symbolism and vaudevillian theatricalism. All four plays reflect the issues of the decade including alienation, ethnicity, changing social mores and the problems caused by confronting change itself. And all of this experimentation was carried out at a time when the audience really cared and when the theatre was a valuable tool in the new game of national definition and interpretation of national concerns. All in all, it was a very good year.

Works Cited

Anderson, John. *New York Post.* 17 Jan. 1925. Package #1. John Howard
    Lawson Papers. Southern Illinois U, Carbondale.
Atkinson, Brooks. *Broadway.* Revised ed. New York: Macmillan, 1974.
Bennett, James O'Donnell. "Our Anniversary, 1907-1924." *The Drama.*
    November 1924: 22/24.
Brockett, Oscar and Robert R. Findlay. *Century of Innovation.* Englewood
    Cliffs: Prentice, 1973.
Dale, Alan. "'Processional Presented by the Guild,'" *American.* 13 Jan. 1925.
    Package #1. John Howard Lawson Papers. Southern Illinois U,
    Carbondale.
Dickenson, Thomas H. "The Paradox of the Timely Play." *Theatre Arts
    Monthly.* November 1924: 723-734.
Durham, Weldon B., ed. *American Theatre Companies: 1888- 1930.* Vol. 2.
    New York: Greenwood Press, 1987.
Eaton, Walter Prichard. *The Theatre Guild: The First Ten Years.* New York:
    Brentano's, 1929.
Gassner, John. *Twenty Best Plays of the Modern American Theatre, Early
    Series.* New York: Crown, 1949.
Hammond, Percy. *New York Tribune.* 25 November 1924. Billy Rose Col-
    lection, New York Public Library.
Hinkley, Theodore B. "War and the Drama." *The Drama.* Nov. 1924: 4.
"The History of What Price Glory?" Souvenir Program. Billy Rose Collec-
    tion, New York Public Library.
Hornblow, Arthur. "Mr. Hornblow Goes to the Play." *Theatre Magazine.*
    November 1924: 15.
Krutch, Joseph Wood. *The American Drama Since 1918.* New York: Ran-
    dom, 1939.
___. "Drama: The God of Stumps." *Nation.* 119 (1924): 578.
Langner, Lawrence. *The Magic Curtain.* New York: Dutton, 1951.

Lawson, John Howard Lawson. *Processional.* New York: Thomas Seltzer, 1925.

Leuchtenburg, William E. *The Perils of Prosperity, 1914- 32.* Chicago: U of Chicago Press, 1968.

Mantle, Burns. *Contemporary American Playwrights.* New York: Dodd, Mead, 1940.

___. "Guild Trots Out its Padded Cell Play." *Cleveland News.* 18 Jan. 1925. Pressbook, Theatre Guild Archives. Yale U, New Haven.

___. "Life Out of Focus is Shown in Latest Production That Came From Diseased Brain." *Denver Post.* Pressbook, Theatre Guild Archives. Yale U, New Haven.

___. "Processional is a Discordant Jumble." *New York Daily* New. 13 Jan. 1925: 16.

Niblo Jr., Fred. "New O'Neill Play Sinks to Depths." *New York* Telegraph. 12 Nov. 1924. Charles Ellis' Scrapbook. Billy Rose Collection, New York Public Library.

Rathburn, Alan. "Tabulated Results of Last Theatrical Season in New York." *New York Review.* 19 Dec. 1925.

Robertson, W. C. "Drama." *Minneapolis Star.* 7 Dec. 1925. Charles Ellis' Scrapbook. Billy Rose Collection, New York Public Library.

Sayler, Oliver M. *Our American Theatre.* New York: Brentano's, 1923.

Sinnott, James P. *New York Telegraph.* 25 Nov. 1924. Billy Rose Collection, New York Public Library.

Stark, George W. *Detroit News.* 29 Mar. 1925. Billy Rose Collection, New York Public Library.

___. "O'Neill Still Full of Gloom: Playwright Reveals Revolting Story of Life on New England Farm." *Detroit News.* 16 Nov. 1924. Charles Ellis' Scrapbook. Billy Rose Collection, New York Public Library.

Wainscott, Ronald H. *Staging O'Neill: The Experimental Years, 1920-1934.* New Haven: Yale U Press, 1988.

Wilson, Edmund. "Comedy, Classical and American." *Theatre Arts Monthly.* Feb. 1925: 73-83.

Young, Stark. "The Play: Triumph at the Plymouth." *New York* Times. 6 Sept. 1924: 14.

Anderson and Odets

and the Group Theater

by Hal Cantor,
Mohawk Community College/SUNY

The recently published autobiographies of Arthur Miller and Elia Kazan and the 1940 journal of Clifford Odets shed new light on theatrical trends and developments during the 1930s. Maxwell Anderson's involvement with the Group Theater, although it lasted only a short time and resulted in the production of a flop, *Night over Taos,* has great symbolic significance when considered in the context of how the two leading playwrights of the 30s influenced each other, were affected by political events, and developed their distinctive styles. For Anderson, the experience may well have contributed to the shaping of his satirical, Pulitzer-Prize- winning play, *Both Your Houses,* and his contemporary verse tragedy, *Winterset;* for the Group, the relationship encouraged the emergence of its most talented playwright, Clifford Odets.

The Group Theater was born of the dissatisfaction of Harold Clurman, Cheryl Crawford, and Lee Strasberg, with the institutionalized offerings of the Theater Guild. Nurtured by the theories of Copeau and Stanislavsky and the techniques of the Moscow Art Theater, the trio "expected to bring the actor much closer to the content of the play, to link the actor as an individual with the creative purpose of the playwright" (Clurman 21).

At the first meeting at the Hotel Meurice on West Fifty-eighth Street and at later weekly meetings at Steinway Hall, the threesome gathered steam and adherents, such as Waldo Frank, Padraic Colum, Franchot Tone, Sanford Meisner, Stella Adler, Ruth Nelson, and Eunice Stoddard. Permitted by the Guild Board to operate as a quasi-independent unit, they seized this opportunity to organize a company that would concentrate on a "new" approach to theatre, one that would be founded on "life values." As their guiding genius, Harold Clurman, eloquently put it,

> The whole bent of our theatre...would be to combine a study of theatre craft with a creative content which that craft was to express...[Our] interest in the life of our times must lead us to the discovery of those methods that would most truly convey this life through the theatre. (31)

It was Clurman's emphasis on developing a unique relationship with contemporary society that differentiated the Group from other experimental acting groups of the time, that drew to it not only theatre people but musicians like Aaron Copland and photographers like Paul Strand. Clurman passionately urged, "We must help one another find our common ground; we must build our house on it, arrange it as a dwelling place for the whole family of decent humanity" (28). This semi-religious zeal took root in actors like Odets and playwrights like Anderson, found fertile ground in doers like Cheryl Crawford and later Elia Kazan.

In the summer of 1931, armed with the Guild's gift of a play by Paul Green, *The House of Connelly*, the three leaders and 28 handpicked actors arrived at a rented country camp in Brookfield Center, not far from Darien, Connecticut, there to work for no salary but room and board, to rehearse and ready for production two plays to open in the fall, and to forge bonds that would make theatre history.

Anderson's first encounter with the Group took place during the winter of 1931. Already he had achieved some notoriety as the coauthor of *What Price Glory*. After further collaborations with Laurence Stallings and Harold Hickerson and a solo domestic comedy, *Saturday's Children*, he "arrived" on Broadway when the Theater Guild produced his verse drama *Elizabeth the Queen*, staring Alfred Lunt and Lynn Fontanne. Two other members of the cast, Morris Carnovsky and Phoebe Brand, invited the successful playwright to attend a meeting sparked by Clurman, then a play-reader for the Guild, and Crawford, its casting director. With Anderson went still another member of the *Elizabeth* cast, Mab Maynard (stage name, Anthony), soon to be his second wife. Anderson must have been stirred by the idealistic speeches he heard, as was a young bit player for the Guild, Clifford Odets. Anderson gave Clurman an unproduced playscript to read, which the latter rejected; even so, when Clurman asked him to help fund the Group's first summer at Brookfield Center, Anderson contributed $1500. Later that summer he gave several hundred more (Clurman 34).

Anderson's generosity with money to friends and family has been well documented elsewhere (Rice 221; Shivers 109-10). But his interest in the Group sprang not solely from his sympathy with its artistic and social ideals. In February of 1931 his marriage of twenty years to Margaret Haskett, which had been deteriorating for some time, ended suddenly when she died of a blood clot. His neighbors at New City had long been aware of his liaison with Gertrude (Mab) Maynard; indeed soon after meeting him, Mab had become his secretary in 1927, typing his plays and handling his correspondence (Shivers 109-13, 120-21).

After Mab's separation from her husband in 1930, Anderson had become her primary means of support even though they did not live together. It is not surprising, then, that Anderson should have rented a house not far from Brookfield Center to be near the stagestruck young actress. (Whether Anderson wangled her a walk-on in *The House of Connelly* or her own wiles did the trick is not clear.) He attended rehearsals and, probably at the behest of the fun-loving Mab, threw frequent parties for the company. He enjoyed their youth, their buoyant high spirits, and particularly savored conversations on the state of contemporary drama with Harold Clurman.

At some point during this magical summer, the older playwright met a flashing-eyed, handsome, impecunious young actor, Clifford Odets; the normally reserved Anderson liked him at once, twice giving him money. Although it was unlikely he was aware that Odets was writing in secret, Anderson told him, "you're not really an actor...you're going to be a playwright" (Brenman- Gibson 202).

Anderson's prescience was appreciated but not reciprocated, since Odets had written to director Philip Moeller, one of his mentors at the Theater Guild, that he had seen *Elizabeth the Queen* and had not believed a word of it. Artistically, they were speaking different languages. Anderson had confided to Clurman his ambition to write epic dramas in verse, "...free of petty naturalism, journalese, concern with ephemeral manners" (Clurman 71). In *Elizabeth the Queen* he had celebrated the acts of heroic individuals who spoke the language of heroes—the exalted language of poetry in which the great plays of the past had been written. In Odets' first, unpublished effort, *910 Eden Street*, a directly opposite view is expressed. The fighter Nick attacks the phoniness of his friends who "run away from Life" and hide in the "incensed rooms" of lofty poetry and arty talk: "while you're making up your minds with pretty words, along comes death, T. B., a bum liver, crazy syphilis...and that's the end" (cited in Brenman-Gibson 199). Though the playwright and the neophyte writer were worlds apart, Clurman played godfather to them both.

Later that year when Anderson invited Clurman to New City and complained that America had produced few heroes worthy of his creative admiration, the director worried over the consequences: "He was seeking his heroes elsewhere, and they would speak a language not of our time and place. I urged, with perhaps more subjective feeling than logic, that heroes must be discovered in the present, or at least in America, and that their language, whether in verse or prose, bear an American stamp" (Clurman 71).

Anderson reacted to these remonstrations. He had been following in *The American Mercury* a series of articles about the semi-feudal civilization

29

in New Mexico and the struggle there during the mid-1840s, when it became an American territory. He crossed a "love and honor" plot out of Racine with this material and, beginning in October, rapidly wrote *Night over Taos,* which he presented to the Group Theater because he felt that a "playwright who gets a chance to write for actors he knows...has a better chance for permanence in the theater—where permanence is so badly needed" (Barrett H. Clark, quoted in Avery xliv). Clurman, who had named Anderson to the Advisory Board of the Group, found himself in an unhappy dilemma. His first impression was that *Taos* was "bookish, contrived, uninspired" (Clurman 72). By then, the Group had had a fairly successful debut with *House of Connelly* and had been less successful with its follow-up production *1931*—by Claire and Paul Sifton. While Anderson impatiently awaited a verdict, Clurman reread the play, decided it was "a playable stage piece" despite his reservations and, especially since the Group had no other script on hand, decided to do it. The play was put into rehearsal under Strasberg's direction while the Group was touring *Connelly* in the winter of 1932. It opened in New York on March 9, 1932, and ran for only 13 performances.

While it is hardly worth lingering over as an undiscovered masterpiece, *Night over Taos* is interesting for what it tells us of Anderson's strengths and limitations. The critics were unanimous in praising the beauty of the costumes and set by Robert Edmond Jones: the interior of the great hall of the Montoya hacienda, with its crucifix and candles, heavy oak table, its barred and deeply embrasured windows (*Second Nights*, Arthur Ruhl, March 13, 1932). Some admired J. Edward Bromberg's interpretation of Don Pablo Montoya, the central figure in this romantic tragedy, while others found his stocky figure and dignified recitations detrimental. (Much later, Bromberg would play a Spanish nobleman with a comic twist in the movie *The Mark of Zorro*.)

All of the critics saw the dramatic potential in the conflict between the last outpost of Spanish power in North American—as embodied by a few rich Mexican landowners in Taos and a powerful priest, Father Martinez—and the United States government. There was drama in the 1847 rebellion in Taos, where the American governor was murdered and where 1000 primitively armed Mexicans and Indians met the forces of the United States Army, which was bent on revenging the murder and subduing the rebels. There was absurdity and courage-in-defeat, to which Anderson added a melodramatic tale of a father with two sons, one of whom betrays him to the invading forces, another of whom steals the love of his intended bride. Don Pablo ends by killing the treacherous son and by magnanimously drinking the poisoned cup which he had intended to give to the lovers. He dies recognizing that the decaying feudal world he represents must give way to Yankee hustle and muscle.

Whatever their reservations may have been about Stella Adler, Morris Carnovsky, Franchot Tone, and Clifford Odets playing Spanish nobles and Mexican peasants, the critics came down hardest on Maxwell Anderson. To a man (and they were all men then) they damned the author with faint praise. Brooks Atkinson's review was typical: "Mr. Anderson has told his story with force and candor and with a respect for the impact of the English language. What makes it a little chilly in the theatre is the predominance of idea over emotion. Although his characters are Spanish and are caught in a moment of high endeavor, Mr. Anderson has told us more of what they think than what they feel, and his drama savors a little of correct university theatre." Robert Garland called it "bookish" and congratulated the Group for "giving the best it has to give to a poetic, historic and all too literary play...." Burns Mantle wrote, "I found it an interesting but unexciting drama." And Richard Lockridge observed that "lacking, somewhere, was the heat that would have fused all the elements into a tempered drama.... The story is told dramatically and sometimes poetically. Only some deep conviction is lacking in Mr. Anderson's writing, so that much of it seems very far away and long ago." Where most of the critics had applauded *Elizabeth the Queen's* use of verse in high drama, now they were praising Anderson's poetic flights with faint damns. One of the more judicious critics, Carl Carmer, thought that Anderson had not "let himself go.... Only in the speeches of Montoya does one feel the kind of hearty full-blown drama that *Night over Taos* should have been. If more of the play had had the quality of the old man's last long speech...it might have won greater distinction."

My own reading of *Taos* and of Anderson's source (*The American Mercury* articles by Harvey Fergusson published in book form as *Rio Grande*) lead me to concur with the critical consensus. The central figures in Anderson's play are wooden stereotypes. Don Montoya's third act suicide seems unmotivated and the playwright has failed to capture the complexity of Father Martinez, a fascinating figure in Fergusson's book, a wily despot who preserves his autocratic rule by opening schools for the peasants and giving lip service to democracy. Anderson's verse passages have a stagey grandeur more suited to Racine than to the rough frontier folk. He permits his love of a "big" historical moment to override his youthful bias toward the democratic left; he sympathizes with the descendants of the *conquistadores*, despite their exploitation of the peasants, and expects his audience will do likewise. The failure of *Taos* left Clurman and Strasberg, its director, with a distaste for heroic verse drama, an aversion they would later regret. When the Group assembled at Dover Furnace, New York for its second summer, the directors had selected two contemporary plays in prose to be rehearsed and offered in the fall. Anderson, who took defeat philosophically, had gone to Hollywood to work on a film script. To relieve the tedium of what he always regarded as hack work, he began to write *Both Your Houses* which, after its successful run in 1933, won him the Pulitzer Prize for Drama.

In the case of a versatile artist like Anderson, speculation about motives is dangerous. He may have turned to satirical prose drama because satire was part of his creative bag of tricks or for a change of pace. But the impulse to write such a scathing denunciation of political corruption and rapacity may have arisen from his close contact in one of the worst years of the Great Depression with the radical mix of Socialist and Marxist activists in the Group Theater. That he gave *Both Your Houses* to the Theater Guild rather than the Group may have been fallout from the fiasco of *Night over Taos*.

Earlier, during that summer at Dover Furnace, Clifford Odets was discovering that, as Anderson had predicted, he was destined to be a playwright. Frustrated by his failure to impress Clurman and Strasberg as an actor, he had plunged ahead with a drama about an individualistic composer based on the career of Beethoven, his role model and all-time hero. On the scene was another well-known writer, John Howard Lawson, working on his play, *Success Story*, which was to be presented by the Group.

At this point there occurred a comic farce worthy of Feydeau. Anderson's mistress, Mab Maynard, brought Odets Anderson's typewriter each night to type the scenes of the Beethoven play (Brenman-Gibson 226). Anderson visited from Hollywood on weekends and by August had completed a draft of *Both Your Houses*; he bought a new ribbon for the typewriter on which Mab presumably typed his Washington satire (Brenman-Gibson 234). By the middle of August, to Odets' chagrin, Mab turned over the typewriter to Lawson for *him* to use in revising *Success Story*. Mab, whom Anderson claimed in marriage in the fall, had been the symbolic midwife to two important plays and one putative playwright during one fertile summer.

For Odets, though, the summer ended on a serious note. Clurman critiqued his fledgling drama and "did not like it"; he later confessed that it struck him as "a very bad play" unlike "the interesting if confused start" of *910 Eden Street* (Clurman 88). He advised Odets to return to "the Greenbaum family play" (Brenman-Gibson 239), the notes for which Odets had shown him earlier. Those notes were transformed that year into the first draft of *I've Got the Blues* which, with further changes, evolved into Odets' first fully mature masterpiece, *Awake and Sing!*

By 1935, the Group's drought was over. The company had had a smash hit in Sidney Kingsley's *Men in White* and, in the new season, presented Odets' *Awake and Sing!* and *Waiting for Lefty*. For his part, Anderson had followed his satire on Washington's graft and corruption with *Mary of Scotland,* another successful verse tragedy for the Theater Guild. In a "round up piece on Anderson for *Theatre Arts Monthly* (June 1933), Carl Carmer had written:

> *Elizabeth the Queen* is the most distinguished play that Anderson has yet written. It is dramatic literature of which America may well be proud.... But this is not enough. Since Maxwell Anderson has reached his playwright's maturity theatregoers have seen no one play in which all of his talents have been concentrated. Like many another dramatist he has

evaded the issue of poetic drama by writing it as if it were out of the past, taking advantage of the convention by which modern audiences give characters in costume special privilege to speak in verse. A play laid in an historic setting cannot best represent the thought and temper of its author's period. And no artist of ambition and faith in himself would shirk the opportunity of speaking not only for himself but for his time. (445-46)

After the failure of Anderson's next play for the Theater Guild, *Valley Forge,* which closed after five weeks (Houseman 142), the pressure on Anderson to write a contemporary verse drama continued. Both Lawrence Avery and Alfred Shivers have noted the gauntlet flung down by Walter Prichard Eaton, a critic and professor at the Yale Drama School, who urged Anderson to write "a poetic drama of modern life" (Avery 45; Shivers 147). When Anderson wrote Eaton that he did not believe great verse could be written in a play on a contemporary theme, Eaton provided him with some lackluster examples (Avery 45-46). It was not until his chance meeting with an old classmate who told him of the madness of the judge who sentenced Sacco and Vanzetti in the notorious 1920 murder trial that Anderson could rise to the challenge. He had written a doctrinaire play on the subject with Harold Hickerson in 1928. Now he had achieved both the necessary aesthetic distance on his subject and confidence in his poetic line to make the attempt. *Winterset* represents Anderson at the peak of his powers and is the play for which he is best remembered. In it, he comes closest to achieving a synthesis between colloquial speech and high romantic verse. Helen Deutsch, a theatrical writer and Anderson's friend, described it this way: "It is not intrusive as poetry; it is a form of irregular unrhymed verse which is pliant, free and admirably suited to the spoken drama" (5). Citing Shadow's speech form Act 1, Scene 1 as an example, Deutsch went on to say, "Never in any of his plays has he sacrificed the theatrical impact of a scene to the beauty of a purple patch. In fact, it is when his scene is most dramatic that his verse is at his best—or it may be said the other way, that his verse is at its best when the material it treats is most dramatic" (5).

Miss Deutsch was writing a Sunday piece introducing the work of her New City neighbor, but, allowing for some hyperbole, what she says is true of *Winterset.* Nowhere else does his verse equal the lyricism of the first meeting between Mio and Miriamne. Trock and Shadow are truly menacing villains and remain so even though they speak in loose iambic pentameter. And Gaunt's Lear-like apostrophes and Esdras' elegiac speech have beauty at dramatic moments. Those who criticize Anderson's use of verse in this play should be forced to sit through the execrable film version of *Winterset* in which his language has been "translated" into prose.

33

After completing *Winterset,* Anderson showed his loyalty as a Group Associate by first offering it to the Group Theater. We may surmise that he identified the Group actors and directors as appropriate sponsors for a play about the aftermath of the Sacco-Vanzetti trial. After all, the Group had staged in the summer of 1934 *Gods of the Lightning* at Green Mansions, New York; Anderson had attended a rehearsal and sympathized with Odets who was acting one of the parts and having difficulty memorizing his lines (Brenman-Gibson 266-67).

Clurman made a serious mistake—which he later acknowledged—by rejecting *Winterset;* he was uncomfortable with what he called its "'Elizabethan' East Side" and, one suspects, his unhappy memories of *Night over Taos.* Clurman would list *Winterset,* the first play to win the Drama Critics' Circle Award, along with his later rejection of William Saroyan's *The Time of Your Life,* as the major misjudgments of his career with the Group (Clurman 147, 264).

But in 1935, the year of Odets' breakthrough, when the Group had achieved "its most memorable and significant accomplishments" (Clurman 134), he might be excused this error. With the Group now on solid ground, Clurman and Cheryl Crawford felt sufficiently secure to travel to the Soviet Union. The traditional summer retreat of the Group was called off, since the Group planned to tour *Awake and Sing!* and *Waiting for Lefty* while it awaited the completion of Odets' *Paradise Lost,* parts of which already had been in rehearsal.

This play which Odets had begun the previous summer and had struggled with for most of the year, was giving the newly-hailed *Wunderkind* a severe case of writer's block. Partly his paralysis sprang from his desire not to repeat the milieu and family types of *Awake and Sing!* Odets wanted to de-Jewisize *Paradise Lost* and make a large statement about American life impacted by the Depression to a broad audience. Partly his slow progress could be traced to personal problems—the enormous demands of the parties, interviews, speaking dates which his new-found celebrity entailed. Inwardly terrified by his own success, he feared that he could not repeat it. Then there was the unexpected death of his mother of peritonitis in May, after which he thought he was having a nervous breakdown and feared he was going insane (Brenman-Gibson 359).

A sympathetic Helen Deutsch invited Odets to New City, where she was staying in a rented studio not far from Mab and Maxwell Anderson. The two of them visited the Andersons, and a violent quarrel between the two playwrights erupted concerning the possibility of a humanist society developing in Soviet Russia. Anderson believed that Russia would soon become "a frank tyranny" and said so. Disturbed and irritated, Odets lost control of himself and shouted at Anderson, "What's bothering you is the income tax, the income tax! You are a damned reactionary, a fascist!" Deutsch was horrified at his attack on her close friends and had to drag the enraged and abusive Odets away as he continued to shout epithets at Anderson from the driveway (Brenman-Gibson 359-60). Odets' biographer believes that Anderson was the object of Odets' repressed rage at his father and also that the incident reveals his disappointment with the progress of events in the Soviet Union. Later he apologized for his behavior in a note to Deutsch, but the rift between the two men was never healed.

In reality both playwrights were politically and temperamentally opposed. Anderson, despite his youthful pacifism and his poem in support of the Russian Revolution, was appalled by Big Government and believed that democracy was preferable simply because it was too inefficient for most corruption to go unnoticed (Shivers 175). Shy and reflective by nature, he shunned the spotlight instinctively. Shortly after his falling out with Odets, he refused to be a sponsor of a fund-raising dinner for the American League Against War and Fascism (at which Odets and others were slated to speak), stating that "although I have an aversion both to war and to fascism, they both seem to me hardy perennials, inherent in the race at its present stage of development, and not to be defeated by propaganda—even their own" (Avery 54). Odets, on the other hand, although he bridled at Communism's suppression of the individual and left the Party in 1935 after eight months, remained Marxist in orientation and, even in the 1940s, a revolutionary spokesman. Volatile and brash, he was active in opposing fascism because the role suited his militant self-image.

Arthur Miller describes a sad coda to Odets' days as a fiery Marxist, when he addressed the Cultural and Scientific Conference for World Peace before an audience that included Dmitri Shostakovich, Aaron Copland, Norman Mailer, Lillian Hellman, Norman Cousins, and Mark Van Doren (237-40). This assembly of noted liberals had gathered to oppose the growing cold war against Soviet Russia, only recently a wartime ally. The audience waited expectantly as Odets rose to speak on the platform. In a whispery voice, Odets began: "Why is there this threat of war?" Then he went on, speaking softly and quietly, asking the group why they had gathered there to protest, why had the politicians failed them, what was the cause of this disharmony among nations. Where-upon he raised his clenched fist and shouted at the top of his voice, "MONEEY!" He paused and began another series of questions. Once again, he screamed out "MONEEEY!" It was the cause of all danger and root of all evil. The distinguished audience tittered and Miller later reflected,

> The point is that we were now in 1949, some fifteen years past Odets' springtide of theatrical rebellion against the failed America of the Depression. Yet not only was he still generally identified with that period, but despite his ten years of Hollywood luxury, he himself evidently felt as he faced this audience that he should sound as though it were

still 1935; helpless before his own past, he felt bound to reidentify himself as "Odets." (236-37)

For all their dissimilarities, Anderson and Odets shared a similar problem: how to break out of the narrow mold of naturalism in the theatre and to embody the American themes Clurman had urged on both of them in the heightened language of poetry. The playwrights of the 1920s—O'Neill, Rice, Lawson—had looked to Europe and expressionism for their release from the well-made play. Anderson and Odets, the dominant playwrights of the 1930s, both sought an organic form that would best express their thematic concerns. Anderson characteristically dealt with heroism, with individualism threatened by brutish forces, and with the search for justice. Odets' favorite themes were the family as a source of strength and weakness—a tender trap, if you will—and the "sell-out" to materialism in a success-crazed society. Anderson treated love as both a high ideal and a grand passion; Odets often portrayed lovers threatened by economic forces. Anderson's imagination was both literary and empathic; Odets' was more personal, nourished by his ethnicity.

By the early 1940s both playwrights had solidified their holds on the theatregoing public and had come up with aesthetic rationales. Beginning with the preface to *Winterset,* "A Prelude to Poetry in the Theater," up to the publication of his Rutgers address in *The New York Times* ("By Way of Preface: The Theatre as Religion"), Anderson had championed the verse tragedy. For him the Greek past was prologue, and there were useful, Aristotelian rules— both aesthetic and moral—to guide the playwright, but essentially the theater was a "religious institution devoted entirely to the exaltation of the spirit of man." As he had explained to a graduate student in 1937, he continued to use iambic pentameter in plays because it combined "the maximum of intensity and elevation with a minimum of artificiality in the theatre" (Avery 59).

Odets did not consciously write verse plays, but he invented a richly metaphoric and colloquial dialogue that had the qualities Anderson extolled: "intensity and elevation with a minimum of artificiality." I have analyzed the elements of Odets' dialogue elsewhere and have made the claim—along with other scholars—that Odets was a poetic playwright (Cantor 146-90). The critic Robert Warshow described that dialogue as follows:

> The events of the play [by Odets] are of little consequence; what matters is the words of the characters—the way they talk as much as the words they say. Odets employs consistently and with particular skill what amounts to a special type of dramatic poetry. His characters do not speak in poetry—indeed, they usually become ridiculous when they are made to speak "poetically"—but the speeches put into their mouths have the effect of poetry, suggesting much

more than is being said and depending for the enrichment of the suggestion upon the sensibility of the hearer. (58)

Although there is scant space to do justice in this essay to the dialogue of either playwright, it may be instructive to juxtapose lines from the Mio and Miriamne love scenes in *Winterset* with the dialogue of Moe Axelrod and Hennie Berger, the lovers in *Awake and Sing!*

Here is Mio expressing rapture after their first kiss:

Why, girl, the transfiguration on the mount was nothing to your face. It lights from within—a white chalice holding fire, a flower in flame, this is your face.

Compare this with Moe pleading his love for Hennie:

Say the word—I'll tango on a dime. Don't give me ice when your heart's on fire.

Here is Mio explaining to Miriamne his alienation:

...You see those lights, along the river, cutting across the rain—? those are the hearths of Brooklyn, and up this way the lovenests of Manhattan—they turn their points like knives against me—outcast of the world, snake in the streets—I don't want a handout. I sleep and eat.

Compare this with Moe's Edenic speech to Hennie:

Paradise, you're on a big boat headed south. No more pins and needles in your heart, no snake juiced squirted in your arm. The whole world's green grass and when you cry it's because you're happy.

Probably to a contemporary ear more attuned to understatement and/or inarticulate groans as the verbal signals of affection, both the speeches from *Winterset* and from *Awake and Sing!* sound old-fashioned. However, the difference between them is profound. Anderson's hero expresses himself grandiloquently, using phrases and metaphors that could not occur to a boy of seventeen; Moe's dialogue is emotionally charged but always in character. As Mabel Driscoll Bailey said of *Winterset*, "It is not dramatic poetry. The poetry and the drama are not fused" (134).

In the search for Form appropriate to their thematic content—a concern which obsessed artists during the 1930s—Anderson and Odets both fell short. Anderson had difficulty with tragic drama after *Winterset;* Odets

37

could not extend the range of his family dramas. In his 1940 journal, Odets acutely diagnosed the problem:

> I don't want to continue writing about Jewish life exclusively if I can help it, but great care must be observed while I move to other fields. It is so easy for the reality of the work to go, so easy to find one sweet morning that you have been handling dead life and straw characters instead of the real and impulsive life which was indigenous to your own nature and feeling content. Some writers, Maxwell Anderson, for instance, make the same mistake when they go from "realistic" drama to "poetic drama. They quickly become dissatisfied with naturalism, find it easy and elemental; they yearn for higher forms of expression, poetic conceptions, nobility of line and purpose—and soon their work is abstract, recondite, high-sounding and dead as an empty bottle. These problems, with all of their ramifications, are now your problems, and you had better tread warily. (87)

It cannot be said that either playwright more than fitfully and partially achieved his high purpose. With the dissolution of the Group Theater after the failure of *Night Music* in 1940, Odets took refuge in Hollywood and, except for sporadic break-outs, remained a prisoner of Beverly Hills until his death in 1963. After writing *High Tor* and *Knickerbocker Holiday,* Anderson threw in his lot with The Playwrights Company. His distrust of centralized government, which was apparent in *Knickerbocker Holiday* and deepened in the late 1940s and into the 1950s during the McCarthy period, made him fear a Communist conspiracy. In essence, he became the theatre's "man of letters" and a darling of the matinee crowd. His verse drama *Key Largo* and war play *The Eve of St. Mark* were made into movies but his reputation had rested on his earlier plays.

For the better part of a decade, as the two playwrights' lives and careers met, crisscrossed and parted, two different and distinct voices contended for preeminence in American drama. Neither writer prevailed. Odets' poetic realism echoes in the plays of Arthur Miller and Tennessee Williams. Anderson's verse dramas have faded and, except for T. S. Eliot and Archibald MacLeish, the genre has gained no adherents. Neither playwright was able to sustain the excitement of what Harold Clurman called "the fervent years."

Works Cited

Books and Articles

Anderson, Maxwell. *Eleven Verse Plays: 1929-1939*. New York: Harcourt, 1940.

Avery, Laurence G., ed. *Dramatist in America: Letters of Maxwell Anderson, 1912-1958*. Chapel Hill: U of North Carolina P, 1977.

Bailey, Mabel Driscoll. *Maxwell Anderson: The Playwright as Prophet*. New York: Abelard-Schuman, 1957.

Brenman-Gibson, Margaret. *Clifford Odets, American Playwright: The Years from 1906 to 1940*. New York: Atheneum, 1981.

Cantor, Harold. *Clifford Odets: Playwright-Poet*. New York: Scarecrow, 1978.

Carmer, Carl. "Maxwell Anderson: Poet and Champion," *Theatre Arts Monthly*, June 1933.

Chinoy, Helen Krich, ed. "Reunion: A Self-Portrait of the Group Theatre," *Educational Theatre Journal*, December 1976.

Clurman, Harold. *The Fervent Years* (1945). New York: Hill and Wang, 1957.

Deutsch, Helen. "A Playwright and Poet." *New York Herald Tribune*. 22 September 1935, 1 and 5.

Fergusson, Harvey. *Rio Grande*. New York: Knopf, 1933.

Houseman, John. *Run-Through: A Memoir*. New York: Simon and Schuster, 1972.

Kazan, Elia. *A Life*. New York: Knopf, 1988.

Miller, Arthur. *Timebends: A Life*. New York: Grove, 1987.

Odets, Clifford. *The Time is Ripe: The 1940 Journal of Clifford Odets*. New York: Grove, 1988.

___. *Six Plays of Clifford Odets*. New York: Random, 1939.

Shivers, Alfred S. *Life of Maxwell Anderson*. New York: Stein, 1983.

Warshow, Robert. *The Immediate Experience*. New York: Doubleday, 1962.

Reviews Cited

(Reviews of *Night Over Taos* were located in scrapbooks of The Billy Rose Theatre Collection, New York.)

Atkinson, Brooks. *The New York Times*, 10 March 1932.
Brown, John Mason. *New York Evening Post*, 10 March 1932.
Garland, Robert. *New York Herald Tribune*, 10 March 1932.
Lockridge, Richard. *New York Sun*, 10 March 1932.
Mantle, Burns. *The New York Daily News*, 10 March 1932.
Ruhl, Arthur. "Second Nights," *New York Herald Tribune*, 13 March 1932.

The Messianic Figure

in American Political Drama: Anderson and After

by Thomas P. Adler,
Purdue University

"Why does [government] not cherish its wise minority?"
Henry David Thoreau, "Civil Disobedience"
"There is no distinctly American criminal class except congress."
Mark Twain, *Gilded Age*
"Democracy is government by amateurs."
Stuyvesant in *Knickerbocker Holiday*

The most characteristic statement by Maxwell Anderson on the relationship between government and those governed appears in his "Preface to the Politics of *Knickerbocker Holiday*" (1938):

> The gravest and most constant danger to a man's life, liberty and happiness is the government under which he lives.... I believe now, that a civilization is a balance of selfish interests, and that a government is necessary as an arbiter among these interests, but that the government must never be trusted, must be constantly watched, and must be drastically limited in its scope, because it, too, is a selfish interest and will automatically become a monopoly in crime and devour the civilization over which it presides unless there are definite and positive checks on its activities. The constitu-

41

tion is a monument to our forefathers' distrust of the state....
(v)

This is not to suggest, however, that Anderson's political philosophy underwent no developmental changes during the tumultuous decade of the 1930s; that it definitely did so receives confirmation, in part, from the alterations he made in the original 1933 version of *Both Your Houses* for its West Coast revival in 1939.

And yet, as both Alfred Shivers, the dramatist's biographer, and Gerald Rabkin, the critic who has addressed this issue most fully, assert, Anderson continued to maintain a leavening measure of pessimism, even cynicism, about the institution of government, regarding it as "the natural enemy of the average citizen" (Shivers 198). If, according to Shivers, Anderson demonstrates always a faith in the individual, he equally, like Emerson and Thoreau, reveals an iconoclastic mistrust of all government—even one democratic in form—which is inherently susceptible to corruption by power and to the violation of libertarian ideals. Nevertheless, in the face of a war against a totalitarian force that itself abrogates liberty, Anderson will come to defend democracy as the "best" possible form of government, "say[ing] that if any harm arises it is from the men who run it" (185). Rabkin finds Anderson radically skeptical of all political authorities and ideologies, because organized government tends to be corrupt and tyrannical; resistance in the name of individual freedom is seen, therefore, as the essential response. However, is not such a stance in itself basically futile, since social evil is immutable and not amenable to correction (264-65)? It is in *Both Your Houses,* his only Pulitzer Prize play, that Anderson openly confronts these issues.

Part I of this study will attempt briefly to situate Anderson's drama of ideas within the context of a few political thinkers and earlier creative artists; Part II will analyze Anderson's 1933 play; Part III will examine three later American works which, if not all directly indebted to *Both Your Houses* appear to carry on from it; and the very brief coda that comprises Part IV will try to hint at why this tradition of the essentially nonsatiric messianic political play has now apparently become at least temporarily dormant.

I

Anderson's *Both Your Houses* implicitly espouses a notion of the electorate not unlike that discovered in the writings of Alexis de Tocqueville and John Stuart Mill, both of whom, while prizing individual conscience and character, sensed that majority rule may mean that mediocrity rules. Tocqueville, who seems to have taken over from religious thought into political philosophy the belief in an "inner light" that guides the individual, knows that the majority opinion may be intolerant of the minority viewpoint in its midst, enforcing conformity rather than independence in thought and action. As he writes in *Democracy in America* (35), "What is a majority, in its collective capacity, if not an individual with opinions, and usually with interests, contrary to those of another individual, called the minority?" (231)

Mill goes even further in his suspicion that collective rule by the majority tends to level everything down to a kind of uniformity, an average that prevents the exceptional from flowering except when a society is willing to permit and nurture an indispensable aristocracy of thought and character. "No government," he claims in *On Liberty* (859), "by a democracy or a numerous aristocracy, either in its political acts or in the opinions, qualities, and tone of mind which it fosters, ever did or could rise above mediocrity, except in so far as the Many have let themselves be guided (which in their best times they have always done) by the counsels and influence of a more highly gifted and instructed One or Few" (62-3). As Maurice Cranston reiterated recently, "Mill was a liberal, but not a democrat.... It was precisely because Mill set such a high value on intellectual and general culture that he mistrusted those who lacked it. He scorned the proletariat" (88-9)—a scorn that will filter down through the plays discussed here. Yet a popular art form such as the drama tends by and large to be conservative in the thrust of its thinking, and so this expressed need for exceptional persons to dictate values to society would seem inevitably to conflict with a theatre audience's predisposition against even well-intentioned individuals if they appear to reject the will and wisdom of the collective majority. One of the tests, then, for a playwright working within the arena of political theatre is precisely how courageous he or she will be in insisting that an audience examine its potential flaws as a citizenry and accept much of the responsibility, even blame, if they are not governed well.

In his "Preface to an Adaptation of Ibsen's *An Enemy of the People*" (1951), Arthur Miller suggests that in an era of fear and suspicion Ibsen's play assumes added weight and significance because it poses

> the central theme of our social life today. Simply, it is the question of whether the democratic guarantees protecting political minorities ought to be set aside in time of crisis. More personally, it is the question of whether one's vision of the truth ought to be source of guilt at a time when the mass of men condemn it as a dangerous and devilish lie.... There never was, nor will there ever be, an organized society able to countenance calmly the individual who insists that he is right while the vast majority is absolutely wrong. (17-18)

Ibsen's John Stockmann stands alone, deserted eventually even by the liberal press, in opposition to a city administration, headed by his brother, that thinks nothing of risking people's physical health for economic gain. In words that express not only Ibsen's sentiment but, as Michael Meyer has pointed out in his definitive biography of the dramatist (507), those of Mill as well, Stockmann states the case for society's need of an intellectual elite, noble in character, spirit, and will, to protect it from the collective mediocrity of majority opinion:

> The most insidious enemy of truth and freedom among us is the solid majority.... The majority is never right, I say, never! ...I think we've got to agree that, all over this whole wide earth, the stupid are in a fearsomely overpowering majority.... The majority has the might— unhappily—but it lacks the *right*. The right is with me, and the other few solitary individuals. The minority is always right. (355-6)

Stockmann rejects both the notion that a ruling class of politicians infallibly knows and attends to the common good, as well as the notion that where one finds power, there also is right.

Eschewing the meekness of Christ, he will recruit as the first disciples for his new order of the "spiritually accomplished...twelve boys...off the street—regular little punks" (385). If there had been an air of envy and vindictiveness about Stockmann's actions all along, he now elevates rejection by the masses and victimization by the few as absolute values. Indeed, his Messiah complex, his need to become a martyr or scapegoat for society, ultimately renders him, as even Ibsen realized, a "muddled" visionary at best, reducing him in the eyes of most contemporary audiences to a serio-comic rather than an unquestionably heroic individual. Nevertheless, if there is a single protagonist and, indeed, one single play that seems to stand behind those under exploration here, it would unquestionably appear to be Stockmann and Ibsen's *Enemy of the People*.

Before deciding to remain in his community, standing virtually alone, Stockmann entertains the option of setting sail for America, although he feels "sure they have a plague of solid majorities and...all the other bedevilments" (368) there as well. That suspicion is amply borne out by a New World work of about the same time, Henry Adams's novel *Democracy* (1880), which Noel Perrin in "Gulliver Goes to Washington" has recently termed "the best political novel yet written in America" (72)—perhaps with a bit of hyperbole when one remembers Robert Penn Warren's *All the King's Men*. Subtitled "An American Novel," *Democracy* might have aptly been called "The Education of Mrs. Lightfoot (Madeleine) Lee," a lonely widow who goes to Washington a cultured naif, only to discover that politics and morality seldom mix. If a democratic form of government has as its ideal "to raise the masses to a higher intelligence than formerly" (40), the reality that Mrs. Lee discovers instead (and which Adams expresses, significantly, through a number of theatrical metaphors) is a "slowly eddying dance of Democracy" (45), outwardly "aping...monarchical forms," inwardly diseased by ambition, dishonesty, and a general meanness that the plethora of animal imagery supports. If Mrs. Lee must see things always in terms of "right and wrong" (39), her antagonist, Senator, later Secretary, Ratcliffe, denies that moral categories can appropriately be applied to practical politics, especially when pursued with a Faustian thirst for power. Madeleine's dalliance with this man who would be president throws her into a moral quagmire, and she can only preserve herself from complete demoralization by escaping to Europe, though she regrets the need to admit, in the novel's last line, that "nine out of ten of [her] countrymen would say [she] made a mistake" (184). Even Ratcliffe can assert non-facetiously that there exists "no chance for Reform as long as citizens stay the same" (33)—that is, so long as the electorate remain as apathetic and asleep as they are in Ibsen's play; furthermore, the putative romance between Ratcliffe and Mrs. Lee contributes a plot strain not found in Ibsen that will assume increased importance in the political plays that follow. One of the novel's characters, Baron Jacobi, predicts that in a hundred years (which would be 1980) governmental abuse will have increased so that "the United States will be more corrupt than Rome under Caligula; more corrupt than the Church under Leo X; more corrupt than France under the Regent!" (383). Little wonder, given such passages as these, that our contemporary playwright Romulus Linney, who adapted *Democracy* to the stage in the 1960s, judges Adams's book "still very modern indeed ...an affectionate, sound, and abiding prophecy" (14).

These four writers—de Tocqueville, Mill, Ibsen, and Adams—together provide a framework by establishing a number of motifs that will reverberate through the four plays discussed below: first, a radical mistrust of the wisdom of the intolerant majority; second, a judgment of the citizenry in a democracy as basically apathetic and uninvolved; third, the need for an aristocracy of character and intellect to lead the multitude; fourth, a messianic leader convinced of the necessity to be a rejected, perhaps even victimized outsider; and fifth, a fear that involvement in government service may inherently be morally corrupting of the individual.

II

Perhaps because he valued his verse dramas so highly, Anderson considered the prose *Both Your Houses* "by all odds his worst" offering (quoted in Toohey, 109). Polemical tract leavened by modest political satire, *Houses* follows the career of a first-term United States congressman. Something of the transparency of the play's moral conflicts is thrust at the audience through the schematic and too-insistent name symbolism. The naive and too good to be true hero-writ-large is named Alan McClean; he is surrounded by a tainted politician but basically good man named Simon Gray and a pragmatic old politico named Solomon Fitzmaurice, who is totally without guile in the sense that he never pretends to be other than what he is. Given that American theatregoers can seldom be counted on to take their politics straight, the play boasts a refreshing turn in that the guy, Alan, does not get the girl, Marjorie, in this instance the daughter of his foe Gray. The tragic possibilities of Alan's moral dilemma—faced as he is with the two equally demanding ethical imperatives of not destroying another human being's reputation while at the same time remaining true to his conscience—receive inadequate emphasis and so dissipate somewhat before play's end. What exists in abundance, however, is an explicit dose of cynicism about the democratic system that faces its greatest challenge because of a less than morally high- minded Congress and a disinterested and apathetic electorate.

Never a regular party man, McClean arrives in Washington a political neophyte, wide-eyed and uncompromising. Son of a newspaperman, wearer of mail-order clothes, and devotee of Thomas Jefferson, he has lost his college job because of his crusading social commitment and now, like an earlier-day Ralph Nader, even orders his *own* election investigation for possible abuses. No deficit spender, he urges fiscal restraint. Assigned to the Appropriations Committee, he discovers that all the other members are out to get something for themselves and their constituents by tacking amendments on to a bill for a dam. Alan's natural instinct to blame the system but maintain his faith in the citizenry seems confirmed by the facts up to this point. Solomon Fitzmaurice, acting partially as Anderson's *raisonneur*, does not, however, hold such a sanguine and complimentary view of the voters. A former radical who speaks frankly about his own motives and about the evils that daily creep into the American system (for example, using taxpayers' money for patrolling the Canadian border to prevent an invasion of Japanese beetles from the Southwest), Solomon displays contempt for those politicians who employ casuistry to cover over their tactics; better to parade one's evil motives openly. An Iago-like rationalist, though not a hypocritical deceiver, he argues that men, politicians especially, should be as the times are. Denying, like Adams's Senator Ratcliffe, that any absolute rights and wrongs rule the actions of those who govern, he personally decides to do right by default, only because doing wrong, in this instance, will not accomplish any narrow self-serving end.

Counseling Alan that reform is not possible, Fitzmaurice argues that it would be preferable to concentrate on the individual virtue of being fully humane, which in this instance pragmatically means not revealing the former questionable dealings of Senator Gray that now threaten to wreck his life. Alan's tactic becomes one of attempting to undermine the system itself by arranging to have so many extra expenditures tacked onto the bill that it will surely invite a Presidential veto. Since the vote is strong enough, however, to override any veto, McClean's scheme backfires. Consequently, Alan in his messianic fervor—one of the other characters derisively refers to him as "this little 'Jesus'" (784)—has accomplished more harm than good: inadvertently,

46

he has taught his unethical colleagues a scheme that will mean even bigger appropriations in the future. Worse than that, he has seen the potential for becoming corrupted himself through making promises in return for votes and has suffered the partial destruction of his idealism. Rationalizing that most seemingly honest people are corrupt and that honesty is perhaps even impossible under the American system, Gray plays the devil's advocate and in doing so receives at least a partial nod of confirmation from the playwright. For Anderson hints that something negative infests the very core of the process, some choice made long ago that is partially responsible for the way of the Washington world: the pragmatic robber barons, embodiments of the height of capitalistic free enterprise, demonstrated that graft could guarantee prosperity— a selling of the nation's soul for financial advancement that O'Neill later in the decade would claim as the "big" theme of his projected cycle, "The Tale of the Possessors Self-Dispossessed." Government is regarded as a taking and a paying-off: sucking from the body politic like a "liver fluke" to feed the politicians, who thrive anyway through bribes and kickbacks from such things as defense contracts that wreck hopes for disarmament. In such a system, money is associated with the right. "God's...in the money" (773)—sounding as though it should be the refrain from one of those Busby Berkeley musical films filled with wonderfully silly and satiric paeans to dollars and cents—has become the watchword of the age.

Anderson follows de Tocqueville and Mill in suggesting that the electorate must be awakened out of their stupor of mediocrity: Solomon claims "no word" or "figure of speech [can] express the complete and illimitable ignorance and incompetence of the voting population" (773). What good, then, is government of, by, and for the people if they, too, insist on acting purely from self-interest? Anderson's "Don Quixote" McClean finally realizes that, far from perfect, this is perhaps not even the best method of government, and that revolution is long overdue. But since neither the complacent voters nor the at-bottom corrupt Congress appears likely to take action to change things, at best Alan can become a pestering gadfly, issuing his jeremiad from the public, if not again from the specifically political, stage. Perhaps Anderson fears permitting the development of an attitude that would make this country susceptible to precisely what he saw beginning to occur in Germany, where a sleeping, apathetic people was awakening to find that the monster in their nightmares was real and that they themselves had helped to create it.

In fact, as Laurence Avery's extensive study of Anderson's manuscript drafts, performance texts, and printed version of *Both Your Houses* reveals, the playwright's awareness of this encroaching threat to democracy actually prompted him to alter significantly Alan's two closing speeches so that they would no longer undermine or question the populace's faith in the institution of democracy itself. The 1939 Alan now asserts:

This is still the best plan for a government ever devised by men! But any government can be wrecked if the people who run it try hard and long enough! Any people can lose their liberties if they sell out for cash so often that it gets to be a business!... You can get away with murder here, and you do. But democracy won't survive in this world if it doesn't survive here, and you're doing your damndest to kill it. You're building a debt that democracy can't survive. You're undermining the morals of every citizen in the country, because in the long run the morals of a country are no better than the morals of those who govern that country (23-24)!

While noting how this new ending is marred by superficiality and by being "inconsistent" with what has come before, Avery regards the decided shift from despair about the possibility of realizing man's highest aspirations to a "qualified hopefulness" as reflective of a "profound change in the attitude" that the dramatist underwent (6)—a shift no less dramatic than that undergone by his fellow member of the Playwrights Company, Robert E. Sherwood, as he moved from the pacifism of *Idiot's Delight* (1936) through the dark night of *Abe Lincoln in Illinois* (1938) to the interventionism of *There Shall Be No Night* (1940).

III

If *Both Your Houses* focuses on politicians already in position of power, Howard Lindsay and Russel Crouse's *State of the Union*, loosely based on Wendell Wilkie's campaign and the Pulitzer winner in drama for 1946, details that rise to power. The emphases in the two works are, nevertheless, virtually identical, though *Union*, more comedic, hits less bullishly. As the coauthors comment, they desired "to stir the conscience of the individual citizen...to say certain things but to do so amusingly" (quoted in Skinner, 200). *Union's* hero, though somewhat less idealistic, ends in virtually the same stance as McClean. Lindsay and Crouse also siphon off much of their indignation, in this case through Mary, the candidate's wife, just as Anderson had through his character Solomon. And both plays involve questions of ambition versus integrity, of public morality versus personal relationships. The word *Union* in the play's title combines a political with a private connotation; the third point in the triangle involving Mary and Grant Matthew is sometimes the political game, and yet it is just as often "the other woman," a big-city newspaper publisher named Kay Thorndike. In fact, the romantic relationship becomes almost more central than the political conflict in this mild comedy of manners.

State of the Union examines in part, as Vidal's *Best Man* later will, the role of the woman behind the political animal. Kay builds up Grant's self-confidence, while Mary—who bemoans the fate of the politician's wife long before it became fashionable to do so—sees her primary function as keeping Grant's ego in check, her worst days being those when he falls prey to the "big man" complex. For Grant is another "Sir Galahad," totally un-tutored in the seamier side of political reality, determined to campaign and win while remaining morally unscathed. Such a "streak of decency" can be a burden since, for the man of conscience, every decision becomes a moral choice. Politics, which initially seems to keep Grant and Mary apart, ironically ends by bringing them closer together as she senses the return of the idealistic boy she wistfully recalls from their honeymoon days. If the campaign turns back the clock on a marriage gone stale, it forces them as well to confront larger ethical issues.

Grant is an unassuming and yet charismatic crusader, not as pure as Alan (he vaguely admits to having paid hush money in the past), but one who continues to maintain faith in the American people and who insists on appeal-ing to their best rather than their worst instincts—refusing, for instance, to trade on the emerging Cold War hatred against the Russians. What does surprise him is the cynicism of the political giants who take advantage of the "lazy...ignorant...prejudiced" people. These lawmakers tend to view politics as a game, and it is in such works as *Union* that the game metaphor so prevalent in the political rhetoric of the 1960s and 1970s first finds expression in American drama. James Conover, the kingmaker, remarks in one of the more obvious occurrences of this metaphor, "In this country, we play politics and to play politics you have to play ball" (222). In the work's somewhat jingoistic ending, Grant finally refuses to cooperate, deciding that he cannot be a candidate on anyone's terms but his own; instead, like Anderson's Alan McClean, he will be a gadfly speaking unhampered from the sidelines. In assuming this role of watchdog, Grant is only doing what every good citizen must, for there can be no such thing as an apolitical stance within a truly democratic society.

In 1953, just prior to the opening of *Tea and Sympathy*, another dramatist named Anderson—this one Robert Woodruff (and no relation to Maxwell)—was invited to join the Playwrights Producing Company, thus making him the only new playwright ever to accept membership after the group's formation. He had long been attracted to Max's work, having written a senior honors thesis at Harvard in 1939 on "The Necessity for Poetic Drama." And when the older Anderson died in 1959, Bob would deliver a eulogy at his funeral, saying in part, "he was that kind of man by which other men are measured. ...one of the leaders of that stunning generation of playwrights who [in the mid-30s] were making our drama the most exciting in the world" (quoted in Wharton, 257-8). In *Come Marching Home* (1946), Robert Ander-son focuses on youthful idealism as it confronts a political reality that demands concessions, and ultimately capitulation, unless the idealist refuses to relinquish his function as conscience of the community and chooses to assume the burden of being stigmatized as an outsider. *Marching*, produced first in California and later off- Broadway and written by a playwright who had not yet had a major production to his name, inevitably suffered by comparison both with *Houses* (which Robert Anderson, despite his admiration for the older Anderson's work, claimed never to have read [personal interview]), and with *Union*, which, while it could not have influenced Anderson, was still running on Broadway when *Come Marching Home* opened.

John Bosworth, formerly a college teacher and writer, "comes marching home" a hero from World War II, receives a tremendous welcome arranged and sponsored by the corrupt yet media-aware State Senator Crawford, and quickly finds himself pitted against Crawford in the next election as a replacement for a candidate killed in an accident. Not political by nature, John's central conflict becomes the pull between his public duty on the one hand and his desire on the other to retreat into a well-deserved private world of wife Toni and home in the country. John's decision to rest on his Navy Cross and divorce himself from public life stems primarily from a disillusionment with a world that does not measure up to the image he developed of it at his father's knee. John's father was incurably, even naively, optimistic; the elder Bosworth literally thought that he could, simply through winning a local election, bring about "the best possible world." Returning home with a vision of war's evil, John now realizes the insufficiency of his father's facile belief. Unwilling to attempt actualizing perfection in and through the social order, John chooses instead the myopically narrower if more comfortably achievable option of withdrawal with wife Toni into a world of their own as a protection against further disillusionment—their personal retrenchment and isolation reflecting how nations often respond after a crisis is overcome. Aware that politics, along with boring him, has an "unattractive" side that downplays truth and exalts self-interest and that would perpetually conflict with his "damndest conscience," John fears what the outcome would be: "an idealist either becomes a cynic or goes crazy" (I, ii, 29).

Ostensibly, the thing that finally sways John to enter the political arena is a series of phone calls just prior to the first act curtain threatening him with bodily harm if he accepts the nomination; working upon him more subtly, however, is the argument of his mentor, Professor Cunningham, who appeals to the remaining vestiges of John's idealism. If he wins office, perhaps he can counteract "all the rottenness, stupidity and greed that runs riot in this country regardless of what some poor little guy may do on a beachhead in Sicily, Italy, France, or Iwo Jima" (I, ii, 35). But while John campaigns to restore the faith of others in the political system, he also risks having his own faith shaken by the nitty-gritty of politics. A neophyte, he goes before the populace "like Don Quixote tilting at windmills," with "no promises, no assurances" (I, ii, 36), believing that the "best man" unfailingly "gets the job" despite the patronage system and that simply telling the truth will be an "inadequate defense against the charge of libel" (II, i, 6, 8).

Not only, however, are many politicians crooked—Senator Crawford, for example, was re-elected after misappropriating funds and is running again even though under indictment for fraud—but the people, through their complacency, contribute to that corruption. John, as Toni tells the audience, thinks that if the people are simply made aware of the rampant abuses they will "overthrow the machine"; John quickly learns, though, that the electorate, jaded by the past ineffectuality of their officials, is "sound asleep." Consequently, he "come[s] to distrust, almost hate the people" (II, ii, 27). In the midst of such a citizenry, John terms himself, in an allusion to Ibsen's drama, "a pillar of society" (III, i, 1). Throughout most of Ibsen's play of that name, Karsten Bernick is a corrupt whitened sepulchre, who only in the closing moments unconvincingly becomes what Bosworth is all along, a bastion of truth.

In fact, the link to Ibsen's Stockmann is much closer. In the abstract, John faces the same danger as Stockmann of becoming an arrogant elitist who regards the mass of humanity with disdain, and this, together with the possibility of becoming so cynical as to fall into absolute negativism, is the chief temptation he must resist. Though he does, like his dramatic forebearer, suffer physical abuse at the hands of the mob, some of whom "rose in righteous indignation because [he] told them they were stupid, criminal and unworthy to be Americans" (II, ii, 28), Bosworth never arrives at such an extreme antidote to society's ills as Stockmann, who finally disbelieves in democracy and arrogantly preaches a gospel of selective breeding—an aspect of Ibsen's character that Miller felt compelled to omit in his post-holocaust, McCarthy era adaptation lest Stockmann seem "racist and fascist" (19).

A more general influence of Ibsen makes itself felt in *Come Marching Home* when John must see the father he worshipped tarnished by the revelation of two secrets: his unscrupulous business deals and his "susceptib[ility] to pretty faces," which is echoed by flaws in John's own past of radical editorials written for his college paper and a minor indiscretion, left annoyingly vague, while drunk and lonely in London during the war. Though he easily passes off threats of blackmail, the conflict finally takes on a sharper focus when it zeroes in on questions of where obligation to self ends and duty to others begins, and what the limits are, if any, of one's social responsibility. When the party decides on election eve that it must withdraw its support and nominate a politically safer candidate, John must choose again between total retreat from the public arena or waging a campaign as an independent, without any hope of winning, with only his wife at his side when he feels "most alone." In opting for the latter course, he, like Mill's and Ibsen's "aristocrats," adopts the messianic role of prophet to his people. As he says in the long political oration that brings the play to its close, "though I shall be defeated, I shall be back year after year.... I shall not be afraid to be a patriot out of season" (III, ii, 18). Nevertheless, as Ibsen also realized, the possibility remains that John will always be "out of

Ibsen also realized, the possibility remains that John will always be "out of season," marching one step ahead of the majority, hoping only that "each year there will be more and more who will understand" (III, ii, 19). If his idealism is no longer as naive or quixotic as it once was, it is still intact, albeit tempered now by experience and solidified by resisting the urge to engage in a too-easy cynicism which would be, after all, only a reverse form of sentimentality.

Although Gore Vidal, unlike Robert Anderson, was never taken into membership in The Playwrights Company, his 1960 drama, *The Best Man*, was not only the last work produced by the group but also one of its biggest commercial successes ever, running for 520 performances, making it their fourth longest running play, after *Tea and Sympathy* (712 performances); Williams's 1955 *Cat on a Hot Tin Roof* (694); and de Hartog's 1951 *The Fourposter* (632). If Anderson's *Come Marching Home* seems the most indebted of the dramas under discussion here to Ibsen's *Enemy of the People*, Vidal's work, subtitled "A Play about Politics," more closely resembles Adams's *Democracy* in the framing of its ethical issues. The play, set during a political convention, focuses on two leading contenders for their party's presidential nomination, and whether they will descend to smear tactics—using rumors of former mental instability and innuendos of homosexual conduct—to destroy one another's chances of reaching that high honor; as Vidal writes in his "Notes," he will employ the structured and symmetrical dramaturgical method of Sardou as filtered through Henry James to construct a play to "demonstrate how, in our confused age, morality means, simply, sex found out. To most Americans, cheating, character assassination, hypocrisy, self- seeking are quite taken for granted as the way things are..." (7-8). Several recent events prove Vidal himself to have been quite prescient—even to having one of the candidates go "to an astrologist...for guidance" (22).

One of those fighting for the nomination is the liberal William Russell, former governor and secretary of state, a witty and intellectual man somewhat akin to Adlai Stevenson who looks upon reform as a means of achieving greater democracy. Although the goal of "government is educating the people about issues" and thus helping to raise them out of their ignorance, "the people in a democracy," on the contrary, "tend to think they have less to fear from a stupid man than from an intelligent one" (15-16). Russell rejects the notion of politics as a popularity contest and decries the use of the speechwriters without convictions of their own who pander to the media that now "sell" not the product but "the image of the product [that is] sometimes...a fake" (17). What gives *The Best Man* greater texture than some of these other plays, especially *State of the Union* to which it is closest in plot, is the characters' willingness to enter into moral discussions having to do with the ends of their actions, rather than simply to focus upon their political shenanigans.

Russell's major competition, Senator Joe Cantwell, comes across in his public actions as a ruthless appeaser, relying on "plain naked ambition"

(43) to get ahead; perhaps insecure because lacking in intellectuality, he decides issues on the basis of expediency, of how well they can be made amenable to his "ends justifies the means" ethic. And yet, personally, he professes a strong belief in God, judgment, and a hereafter: "If I didn't think there was some meaning to all of this I wouldn't be able to go on. I'm a very religious guy, in a funny way" (72). Former President Art Hockstadter, slyly positioning himself in the role of kingmaker while dying from cancer, grudgingly admits that the "age of the Great Hicks [such as himself] is over" (43) and that the time of the Eastern intellectual axis seems to have dawned. Hockstadter counters not only Cantwell's private beliefs but his ends-based ethic as well. Feeling a metaphysical angst over this meaningless handful of dust that is man and the universe, he proposes action over reflection, the means and not the end; the "how" you do things, and not some ideal course of action, is all that matters. Like Adams's Ratcliffe, Hockstadter believes that a strong president must, of necessity, be "immoral." A "saint" does not necessarily make a good leader; in fact, too heavy a dependence upon conscience as a measuring stick may indeed be a drawback. Originally ready to throw his support to Cantwell as someone who would be strong in his use of power in ways that Russell apparently would not, he finally decides to remain neutral, not because of his divergent religious beliefs, but because Cantwell shows himself "stupid" in his inability to understand character.

Russell, who grounds his humanistic system of belief in faith in man and not God, displays a more traditionally developed moral conscience than either Cantwell or Hockstadter; hating the "necessary" deceptions that acting in the political arena entails, he sees himself, like Adams's Madeleine Lee, being sucked into compromise and corruption simply by wanting the power that would come with the presidency. Believing that life is a series of choices, with one good act setting off a chain of others, and that one's only claim to immortality is to "try to be good even when there is no one to force [you] to be good" (168), he refuses to stoop to his opponent's tactic and use the available testimony to libel Cantwell's private life. But neither, however, can he allow Cantwell, who lacks utterly any "sense of right or wrong" (151), to become president, and so he throws his support behind another contender who is then assured of the nomination.

The nominee, Governor Merwin, is, of course, *not* "the best man"—clearly, Russell would have been—but then Vidal's intended implication is that seldom does the best person, either intellectually or morally, have much hope of winning nomination and election. Since "the light blinds us...and we're all afraid of the dark" (168), grayness is likely to hold the day. In the public realm, then, there exists a sense of defeat: neither the people nor politics is likely ever to change, and the age of embracing the potential messiah/saviours who periodically spring up in our midst is over. Yet in the purely private realm, however, things conclude quite differently, for *Best Man* is after all, like *Come Marching Home* and *State of the Union*, at least part romantic comedy. Russell, who formerly has been "athletically promiscuous" because, the audience is led to conclude, of a somewhat sexually distant spouse, reaches an accommodation with his wife who will now settle for little in their autumn years. So on that basis alone Russell can claim that "the best man won" after all. Except for his active support of Merwin's campaign, this will mean, in essence, a retreat from the public into the private arena, with nothing left of the gadfly role as conscience of the people that Alan McClean, Grant Matthews, and John Bosworth had vowed to embrace. It seems, in fact, a retreat hardly less decisive than Madeleine Lee's at the end of *Democracy* had been.

IV

To survey American political drama since 1960 is to find the "serious" being supplanted by the "satiric:" 1967 saw, for example, Barbara Garson's *MacBird*, complete with Lady MacBird, Ten Ken O'Dunc, the Earl of Warren, and Wayne of Morse; Robert J. Myers came along in 1973 with his *Tragedy of Richard II*, subtitled "The life and times of Richard II, King of England, Compared to those of Richard of America in His Second Administration" and featuring Queen Pat, the Bishop of Graham, Lord Kissinger, and Sir George of Bush; and 1984 greeted Elizabeth Swados and Garry Trudeau's musical revue, *Rap Master Ronnie*. Political satire is, of course, nothing new to (or on) the American stage. It formed very much a part of the theatrical scene when Anderson wrote *Both Your Houses*, which won the drama Pulitzer only a year after the George Kaufman, Morrie Ryskind, and Ira and George Gershwin musical *Of Thee I Sing* had. *Houses* shared the boards in 1933 with a sequel by the same team, *Let 'Em Eat Cake*, and five years later Anderson himself, together with composer Kurt Weill, contributed *Knickerbocker Holiday* to the genre.

Originally, Anderson intended *Houses* as a "blast at the Hoover administration;" production delays until after Roosevelt took office meant, however, a decided loss in "topicality" and satirical thrust (Shivers 125), and to anyone looking back at the play through today's jaded lenses the political characters are hardly too outrageously bad enough to seem true. The same might be said also to *The Best Man*, Vidal's comment in the preface about "us[ing] the theater as a place...to satirize folly" (9) notwithstanding. Indeed, when the evil appears no longer curable by anything short of massive upheaval, when despair over the possibility for effecting change becomes widespread, then the mocking laughter of satire (which, as everyone knows, never changes anything but only allows writers to have a rollicking good time while Rome burns) seems the last resort of thinking [wo]men. Moreover, the most receptive audience for political (or, for that matter, any) satire, which tends to position the evil securely in the other fellow and not in the self, will likely be the already converted—or the genial but hopelessly obtuse who laugh at what they do not understand.

What, then, does the virtual disappearance of the messianic figure from American political drama of the past three decades betoken? Not necessarily, it seems safe to conclude, any decided shift to an apolitical stance that would isolate contemporary American dramatists even further from the tradition of classic American authors such as Hawthorne in *The Scarlet Letter* or Melville in *Billy Budd* or Thoreau in "Civil Disobedience" or Twain in *Huckleberry Finn* who, either implicitly or explicitly, have always included a generous dose of political theory, particularly as it pertains to questions of individual freedom vis-a-vis the social contract, to the tension between the exercise of human conscience and the dictates of the law, in their writings. While it may be true that the best American playwrights of today are not as overtly political as, for example, Brenton (*Weapons of Happiness*) or Edgar (*Destiny*) or Cartwright (*Road*) in Britain, oblique political references are still very much a part of the texture of their dramas. How better can one explain, for instance, the exhumed skeleton of Shepard's *Buried Child* than as Vietnam come back to haunt our dulled consciences; or the break-in to steal a list of names in Mamet's *Glengarry Glen Ross* than as Watergate revisited to force home the depth of our moral vacuity?

Even these two examples, however, are more in keeping with the somewhat despairing attitude of recent satirical plays rather than the position of the messianic political dramas which came down—firmly at first albeit finally more mutedly—on the side of possibility. In that, they were simply carrying forward, perhaps desperately, the idealistic belief held by authors such as Thoreau that character and intellect could make a difference and even be contagious. Yet to trace chronologi- cally the social philosophy of these plays from *Both Your Houses* in the early 30s through *State of the Union* and *Come Marching Home* in the mid-40s to *Best Man* at the end of the 50s is to see, as John Wharton claims, a diminution in precisely this time-honored liberal faith in "people['s] capab[ility] of improvement" (263). Their Messiahs find the multitude largely deaf to their messages, any committed rhetoric in an age of image manipulation sounds largely suspect, and serious political drama largely retreats from being any longer a weapon.

Works Cited

Adams, Henry. *Democracy: An American Novel* in *Novels, Mont Saint Michel, The Education*. New York: The Library of America, 1983.

Anderson, Maxwell. *Both Your Houses* in *The Pulitzer Plays* 1918-1934. Ed. Kathryn Coe and William H. Cordell. New York: Random, 1935.

___. *Knickerbocker Holiday*. Washington, D.C.: Anderson House, 1938.

Anderson, Robert. *Come Marching Home*. Unpublished playscript, 1946.

___. Personal interview, 4 June 1974.

Avery, Laurence G. "Maxwell Anderson and *Both Your Houses*," *North Dakota Quarterly* 38.1 (Winter 1970): 5-24.

Cranston, Maurice. "John Stuart Mill and Liberty," *The Wilson* Quarterly 11.5 (Winter 1987): 82-91.

De Tocqueville, Alexis. *Democracy in America*. Trans. George Lawrence. New York: Harper, 1966.

Ibsen, Henrik. *An Enemy of the People* in *The Complete Modern* Prose Plays. Trans. Rolf Fjelde. New York: New American Library, 1978.

Lindsay, Howard and Russel Crouse. *The State of the Union* in *50 Best Plays of the American Theatre*, vol. 3. New York: Crown, 1969.

Linney, Romulus. "Political Recommendations," *Hungry Mind* Review 8 (Summer 1988): 14.

Meyer, Michael. *Ibsen: A Biography*. Garden City, NY: Doubleday, 1971.

Mill, John Stuart. *On Liberty*. Ed. David Spitz. New York: Norton, 1975.

Miller, Arthur. *The Theater Essays*. Ed. Robert A. Martin. New York: Viking, 1978.

Perrin, Noel. *A Reader's Delight*. Concord, NH: UP of New England, 1988.

Rabkin, Gerald. *Drama and Commitment: Politics in the American Theatre of the Thirties*. Bloomington, IN: Indiana UP, 1964.

Shivers, Alfred S. *The Life of Maxwell Anderson*. New York: Stein, 1983.

Skinner, Cornelia Otis. *Life with Lindsay and Crouse*. Boston: Houghton, 1976.

Toohey, John L. *A History of the Pulitzer Plays*. New York: Citadel, 1957.

Vidal, Gore. *The Best Man: A Play about Politics.* Boston: Little, Brown, 1960.

Wharton, John F. *Life Among the Playwrights: Being Mostly the Story of The Playwrights Producing Company, Inc.* New York: Quadrangle/New York Times, 1974.

Maxwell Anderson's Rules

of Playwriting and Their Use in His Plays

by Randall J. Buchanan,
Texas A & I University

M axwell Anderson began his playwriting career in 1923 with *White Desert*. From that time until his death in 1959, he wrote over 40 plays, ranging from outright failures to glowing successes. Starting in 1935 with the publication of the preface to *Winterset*, Anderson wrote a series of critical essays that give a fairly complete discussion of his dramatic theories. It is clear that these theories did not spring full-blown from Anderson's head, for he wrote in 1941 concerning his entrance into the theatre,

> I was a journalist, and I knew nothing about the theatre except casually from the outside. But I wrote a verse tragedy, being bored with writing editorials, and a gallant producer put it on the stage—for no reason that I can see. It failed quietly, as it deserved, but after its production the theater tugged at me, its rewards dazzled me—and I wrote other plays, some of then successful. However, from the very beginning the theater was to me, in some fundamental ways, an exasperating puzzle. Some plays succeeded, some did not, and why, nobody knew. Success on the stage seemed to be one of the ultimate mysteries. Leaving aside the questions of acting and directing, the problems of theme, story and writing appeared more confused when discussed by the professors of playwriting. I developed a theory which still looks cogent to me—that a playwright's first success was always largely accidental. After that he could analyze what he had done, and begin to develop an intuition that would

take him through the maze of difficulties and dangers his
action and dialogues must tread. But intuition is an unreli-
able guide, and I was not as intuitive as some others. I
needed a compass—or a pole star—or some theory of what
the theater was about, and I had none. (Off Broadway 23-24)

That Anderson did not trust his own intuition is evidenced by the fact
that the next few plays he wrote were in collaboration, first with Laurence
Stallings and later with Harold Hickerson, both of whom were probably just
as inexperienced as Anderson considered himself to be. Also during this same
period Anderson dramatized the writing of others. The first play that is completely Anderson's is *Saturday's Children*, produced in 1927 (Childs 482). The
question arises as to when Anderson began to develop his own rules or theories
for writing plays. Allen G. Halline wrote,

I believe it was not until the middle 1930s that Anderson
started evolving the theory to which he has given expression
in recent years. One reason for so believing is that not until
1933, in *Mary of Scotland,* did Anderson write a play which
fully measured up to the theory of tragedy he set forth in
1938. If Anderson is like most writers, he created the work
first and theories afterward as to what he had done. (63-64)

It is fairly evident that for at least ten years after Anderson began
writing plays he gave no indication of just what his dramatic theories were,
for Barrett H. Clarke, in 1933, stated that Anderson had never been interviewed
and that, aside from his published or produced work, there was almost nothing
to attribute to Anderson concerning his dramatic theories (4). The preface to
Winterset gives the first published indication of just what Anderson's views of
drama encompass.

In his first critical essay, "Poetry in the Theatre,"Anderson makes
several points concerning his theory of drama. He states that the "playwright
must pluck from the air about him a fable" that is of immediate concern and
interest to the playgoer, and this "fable"must be presented in such a fashion
that it will be acceptable to his neighbors. By 1935, at any rate, Anderson was
realistic about the producing theatre, for he says further, "There is no instance
in the theater of a writer who left behind him a body of unappreciated work
which slowly found its public..." (*Off Broadway* 47). The playwright then,
according to Anderson, must write for that time and place if he is to succeed.
But Anderson does not disregard the aesthetic approach to drama, for he states
further in that essay

that the playwright will also try to make that fable coincide
with something in himself that he wants to put into words.

60

> A certain cleverness in striking a compromise between the world about him and the world within has characterized the work of the greatest as well as the least successful playwrights, for they must take the audience with them if they are to continue to function. (47)

According to Anderson this does not in any way compromise the position of the playwright as an artist, and this statement is not "blasphemy"; for if a playwright does not take the audience into consideration, the end product is left completely to chance, "and a purely chance achievement is not an artistic one"(*Off Broadway* 48).

At the same time Anderson is not setting himself up as a complete judge of what an audience wants, likes, dislikes, or is ready for. That he was not able to do this is evidenced by the fact that throughout his playwriting career he had his share of failures. He says in "Poetry in the Theatre," "Nobody has ever known definitely what any audience wanted."The playwright must make a choice among "imponderables."Still, once his choice is made, the playwright who has more than intuition is indeed fortunate. The playwright who suppresses his other preferences and merely writes what he thinks the audience wants, going completely in that direction, "thinks more of his job than his fame" and is therefore playing it safe (48). Anderson has said, then, that the playwright must constantly compromise between two ideas: (1) what he believes the audience wants, and (2) his own personal preferences of what he believes the audience should want. This compromise is often fraught with perils. The main peril that Anderson sees is the inclination on the part of the playwright to believe that "the public is ready for a theme only because [the playwright] wishes to treat it—or ready for a dramatic method only because he too wished to employ it"(48).

All during his career as a playwright, Anderson wrote and spoke about the need for a poetic theatre: "When I wrote my first play, *White Desert,* I wrote it in verse because I was weary of plays in prose that never lifted from the ground"(*Off Broadway* 53). "I have a strong chronic hope,"he added, "that the theater of this country will outgrow the phase of journalistic social comment and reach occasionally into the upper air of poetic tragedy. I believe with Goethe that dramatic poetry is man's greatest achievement on this earth so far…"(48). Just how keenly Anderson felt concerning the need for poetry in the theatre he expressed in that essay:

> None of the prose moderns, not Synge, not O'Casey, not O'Neill, not Shaw himself, has written anything which we can set unquestionably beside *Oedipus the King* or *Macbeth* or many others we can pick up in the library—and the reason for that is a fairly simple one. Our modern dramatists are not

poets, and the best prose in the world is inferior on the stage
to the best poetry. (5)

Anderson indicates that prose is the language of information and poetry is the
language of emotion. Any prose must be stretched to convey the emotion
desired, and in some very exceptional individuals, such as Synge or O'Casey,
the prose rises to "poetic heights by substituting the unfamiliar speech rhythms
of an untutored people for the rhythm of verse"(50). In most cases, however,
prose under the stress of great emotion breaks down on the stage as it does in
real life into inarticulateness. This leads, Anderson states, to the "cult of
understatement, hence the realistic drama in which the climax is reached in an
eloquent gesture or a moment of meaningful silence"(50). Only through poetry
can the theatre be lifted from the "journalistic phase" spoken of before. This
is Anderson's belief, and, as is seen later in this study, he wrote the majority
of his most successful and apparently most enduring plays in poetry.

The question now arises as to why poetry was so essential to
Anderson's conception of the theatre. The answers can be seen in another
statement in "Poetry in the Theater":

> ...I believe with the early Bernard Shaw that the theater is
> essentially a cathedral of the spirit, devoted to the exaltation
> of men, and boasting an apostolic succession of inspired
> high priests which extends further into past than the Chris-
> tian line founded by St. Peter.... Lately it has recognized the
> mysteries only as a sideshow, and has been overrun with
> guides who prove to an eager public that all saints are plaster
> and all prophets fakes. (48-49)

Anderson believes that the state, despite the steady diet of "journalistic"plays,
is still a cathedral, and that it will change, and once again it will house the
"mysteries":

> An age of reason will be followed once again more by an
> age of faith in things unseen.... What faith men will then
> have, when they have lost their certainty of salvation
> through laboratory work, I don't know, having myself only
> a faith that men will have faith. But it will involve a desire
> for poetry after our starvation diet of prose I have no doubt.
> (51)

The reason Anderson states that mankind would turn to poetry is his belief that
despite the numerous inventions of modern times we have not been altered, so
that we are still lonely and frightened creatures, and that although science has

answered a few questions for us "in the end science itself is obliged to say that the fact is created by the spirit, not the spirit by the fact"(51-51).

Anderson states in "Poetry in the Theater" that "poetic tragedy had never been successfully written about its own place and time"(53). With this in mind, and having experienced failure with *White Desert,* written in verse in 1923, he wrote his next verse plays about historical subjects, not returning to modern themes in verse until *Winterset* in 1935. In writing *Winterset* Anderson fully realized that he was attempting to establish a new theatrical convention and that in so doing he was deliberately risking failure. However, this did not seem too important to him. Of much greater importance was his attempt to create poetic drama containing contemporary comment. As he himself noted, "Whether or not I have solved the problem in *Winterset* is probably of little moment. But it must be solved it we are to have a great theatre in America. Our theatre has not yet produced anything worthy to endure—and endurance, though it may be a fallible test, is the only test of excellence"(54).

In 1937 Anderson gave the Founder's Day address at Carnegie Institute. This address later was published as "What Ever Hope We Have." In this essay Anderson notes very little concerning his guides to playwriting. He does say, however, that it is the aim of the artist to set his vision of the world in "a series of picture writings which convey meaning beyond the scope of direct statement."And he says that all communication is by way of symbols of some kind "because the things an artist has to communicate can be said only in symbols, in the symbols of his art" (17-18). No playwright can merely give his audience his ideas in a bald statement, for this is not the means of communication that is most effective. In any abstract medium the ideas expressed seldom, if ever, are concretely stated; they are stated in a symbolic way, in terms that others comprehend (17-18).

Anderson states further his feelings on what art is supposed to accomplish:

> The dream of the race is that it may make itself better and wiser than it is, and every great philosopher or artist who has ever appeared among us has turned his face away from what man is toward whatever seems to him most godlike that man may become. (20)

The playwright, therefore, must not attempt to depict mankind as we are now but rather as we should be, as we dream of becoming.

In the essay originally entitled "Yes, By the Eternal"and later retitled "The Uses of Poetry,"Anderson expresses this idea again:

> For what the poets are always asking for, visioning, and projecting is man as he must and will be, man a step above and beyond his present, man as he may be glimpsed on some

horizon of dream, a little nearer what he himself wished to become. (*Off Broadway* 91)

He goes on to say that the message of tragedy is "victory in defeat,"that even in death the human spirit can rise to new heights and a greater glory by "a man's conquest of himself in the face of annihilation (90).

These statements concerning the purpose of the art of the theatre contained in the above essays are an indication of Anderson's further thinking on an earlier statement made in "Poetry in the Theater": that the aim of the theatre is the exaltation of men. It is not the purpose of poetry (or the theatre) to attempt to reorganize the scientific or practical world of men; that a good play or good poetry might sometimes be animated by an attack on an existing order, Anderson does not dispute. Yet he adds, "But satire at its best is second or third best...."And, therefore, satire is not and cannot be great theatre or great poetry (*Off Broadway* 88).

In 1938 Anderson wrote one of his most important essays on theatre, "The Essence of Tragedy." It was first delivered to the Modern Language Association in New York in January of that year. Here he clarifies some of his previous statements and makes some illuminating comments in addition. The opening remarks give a clear indication that he is not setting himself up as the final word but that from his experience as a dramatic poet he has determined some elements that might be of use to others:

> Anybody who dares to discuss the making of tragedy lays himself open to critical assault and general barrage, for the theorists have been hunting for the essence of tragedy since Aristotle without entire success. There is no doubt that playwrights have occasionally written tragedy successfully, from Aeschylus on, and there is no doubt that Aristotle came very close to a definition of what tragedy is in his famous passage on catharsis. But why the performance of a tragedy should have a cleansing effect on the audience, why an audience is willing to listen to tragedy, why tragedy has a place in the education of men, has never to my knowledge, been convincingly stated. I must begin by saying that I have not solved the Sphinx's riddle which fifty generations of skillful brains have left in shadow. But I have one suggestion which I think might lead to a solution if it were put to laboratory test by those who know something about philosophical analysis and dialectic. (Essence 3)

Anderson then discusses his own entrance into the theatre and his search for the guides and rules previously mentioned. He confides, "It was not until after I had fumbled my way through a good many successes and an appalling number of failures that I began to doubt the sufficiency of dramatic instinct,"and he also says that he began "to wonder whether or not there were general laws governing dramatic structure which so poor a head for theory as my own might grasp and us"(4). Anderson states that each play is a new problem that presents itself only as it is in the process of being written and that there are so many rules, landmarks, and pitfalls laid down by well-known handbooks on play structure that it is nearly impossible to make one's way through the maze (4).

In this light Anderson begin his search for rules or guides to aid him. Although it is not known exactly when he began this search or when he started applying specific rules to his playwriting endeavors, search and find them he did. Anderson gives his definition of a play in these words: "A play is almost always, probably, an attempt to encapture a vision for the stage" (*Off Broadway* 57). At the same time he presents one of the rules he had discovered, that a playwright must have a vision (termed earlier "a fable"), and must check it carefully before he can assume that it is the type of vision that will make a play. He explains,

> I shan't trouble you with the details of my search for a criterion, partly because I can't remember it in detail. But I reread Aristotle's *Poetics* in the light of some bitter experience, and one of his observations led me to a comparison of ancient and modern playwriting methods. (*Essence* 5)

Rereading the *Poetics* led Anderson to a realization of one of the most important elements of playwriting: the recognition scene. He states that he came to the conclusion that this recognition, as isolated by Aristotle, is generally "an artificial device, a central scene in which the leading character saw through a disguise, recognized as a friend or as an enemy...some person whose identity had been hidden.... There is an instant and profound emotional reaction..."(6). Looking further into Greek drama, Anderson discovered that occasionally "the recognition turned on a situation far more convincing, though no less contrived."On these occasions, as in *Oedipus*, the effect of the recognition on the individual an on the play determines the entire course of action thereafter (6). On this point, Anderson noted,

> I still think that the rule which I formulated for my own guidance is more concise than any other, and so I give it here: A play should lead up to and away from a central crisis, and this crisis should consist in a discovery by the leading character which has an indelible effect on his thought and emotion and completely alters his course of action. The leading character, let me say again, must make the dis-

covery; it must affect him emotionally; and it must alter his direction in the play. (*Off Broadway* 59)

Anderson felt that many of the recognition scenes of the Greeks are obvious and contrived, but when he looked carefully into the plays of Shakespeare and the memorable plays of the moderns, he found the same recognition scenes, only subtler and more difficult to discern. These scenes, Anderson felt, are always there in the plays we choose to remember. The scene does not, in the best plays, deal with the discovery of identity or disguise but "the mainspring in the mechanism of a modern play is almost invariably a discovery by the hero of some element in his environment or in his own soul of which he has not been aware—or which he has not taken sufficiently into account"(*Off Broadway* 59). Anderson states that this scene is so important that the playwright in checking his "vision" must insure that this scene is paramount:

> If the plot he [the playwright] has in mind does not contain a playable episode in which the hero or heroine makes an emotional discovery, a discovery that practically dictates the end of the story then such an episode must be inserted—and if no place can be found for it the subject is almost certainly a poor one for the theater. If this emotional discovery is contained in the story, but is not central, then it must be made central, and the whole action must revolve around it. (*Off Broadway* 61)

The next element which Anderson discusses is the leading character: "The hero who is to make the central discovery in the play must not be a perfect man. He must have some variation of what Aristotle calls a tragic fault..."(61). After having made his discovery the hero must be able to change in himself and in his actions. The leading character goes through some type of experience that will enable him to open his eyes to some fault or error of his own (61). The audience, watching a play, may not be able sufficiently to identify themselves with a man who was without fault or error or possibly of realization. Therefore, the hero must not be a perfect man in order that he may experience discovery or recognition.

The next logical step in the development of Anderson's rules, as stated in "The Essence of Tragedy,"is that the leading character, after making the discovery, must become a better person than he was previously:

> When he makes his discovery he must change both in himself and in his action—and he must change for the better. The fault can be a very simple one—a mere unawareness, for example—but only for the worse, and for a reason which

I shall discuss later, it is necessary that he must become more admirable, and not less so, at the end of the play.... He must learn through suffering. (61)

Anderson warns the playwright against trying a reversal of the formula, in which the hero makes a discovery that affects him in an evil way or in a manner which the audience interprets as evil. Anderson continues this discussion by stating that an audience will always demand that any alteration in the character of "the hero be for the better—or for what it believes to be the better"(*Off Broadway* 62). Anderson, as I have said before, is realistic concerning an audience and, therefore, the meanings of plays change with the changing attitudes of audiences over the centuries:

> One thing only is certain; that an audience watching a play will go along with it only when the leading character responds in the end to what it considers a higher moral impulse than moved him at the beginning of the story, though an audience will, of course, define morality as it pleases and in the terms of its own day. It may be that there is no absolute up or down in this world, but the race believes that there is, and will not hear of any denial. (*Off Broadway* 62-63)

I have earlier asserted that the aim of poetry and especially dramatic poetry is the exaltation of man. Anderson returns to this same thought when he says, "From the point of view of the playwright, then, the essence of tragedy, or even of a serious play, is the spiritual awakening, or regeneration of his hero" (*Off Broadway* 64). This also echoes a statement he made earlier in this same regard, that the hero of a play must come out of the experiences a better person than he previously was.

The belief that in the essential modern drama is not greatly altered from that of the days of Sophocles and Euripides leads to another of Anderson's rules, that in establishing a play's core of meaning for an audience, a playwright must follow in the essentials the same pattern set out by the ancient writers of Attica. As Anderson puts it,

> However unaware of it we may be, our theater has followed the Greek patterns with no change in essence, from Aristophanes and Euripides to our own day. Our more ribald musical comedies are simply our approximation of the Bacchic rites of Old Comedy. In the rest of our theater we some times follow Sophocles, whose tragedy is always an exaltation of the human spirit, sometimes Euripides, whose

tragicomedy follows the same pattern of excellence achieved through suffering. (*Off Broadway* 63-64)

In Anderson's few comments on comedy it is apparent that he felt the same about comedy as he did about tragedy, that modern theatre still follows the Greek model, that of the Greek new comedy. And he felt that it differs from tragedy in one respect mainly, that it offers a happier scene and puts its hero through an ordeal or a test that is less than lethal (64). That comedy differs from tragedy mainly in this respect can also be considered one of Anderson's rules or guides to dramatic composition.

Anderson seems to have answered, at least to his own satisfaction, his question as to why an audience was willing to listen to tragedy. The answer seems to lie in Anderson's feeling that an audience goes to the theatre, especially to view a tragedy, to reaffirm its faith in itself and in mankind.

There is one more concept of theatre that Anderson put forth in "The Essence of Tragedy" which it would be well to consider at this time: "that the theatre at its best is a religious affirmation, an age-old rite restating and reassuring man's belief in his own destiny and his ultimate hope"(66). Anderson already considered the theatre as a cathedral, and now he calls drama a religious affirmation. He expressed himself more completely on this subject in the essay "Off Broadway." Whether this was a new idea to Anderson in 1938 when "The Essence of Tragedy" was first written, is unknown, but is worthy of note at this time.

In October, 1941, Anderson delivered a lecture at Rutgers University that was published in *The New York Times* under the title "By Way of Preface: The Theatre as Religion." This essay forms the title essay of the volume *Off Broadway* which was published in 1947. In the essay "Off Broadway" Anderson summarizes some of his rules or guides for playwriting. Anderson also states that these rules or essentials in playwriting apply not only to the plays that we consider extraordinary but to all plays and just as much to our modern plays as to plays by Shakespeare or Jonson (24-26):

> The theatrical profession may protest as much as it likes, the theologians may protest, and the majority of those who see our plays would probably be amazed to hear it, but the theater is a religious institution devoted entirely to the exaltation of the spirit of man. It has no formal religion. It is a church without creed, but there is no doubt in my mind that our theater, instead of being as the evangelical ministers used to believe, the gateway to hell, is as much a worship as the theater of the Greeks, and has exactly the same meaning in our lives. (28)

That this idea was not part of Anderson's original philosophy of the theatre is obvious because he says, "When I first wrote plays this statement would have seemed incredible to me"(28). He further says that if one examines the matter that is sold in the theatre this idea is not so difficult to believe, for "The plays that please most and run longest in these dusty alleys are representative of human loyalty, courage, love that purges the soul, grief that ennobles"(28). Clearly Anderson means that the true and underlying purpose of the theatre is to discover and to hold up to the regard of its audience that which is most admirable in the human race (27). Anderson holds that a playwright, more than any other writer or any other artist, must have something intelligible to say in everything he puts before the public. The audience will demand that a play must take an attitude toward the world, and for that the playwright must have some type of convictions:

> But if he is going to put plays on the stage he must have at least fragmentary convictions. Sometimes his convictions are subconscious; sometimes they are inherited. Sometimes the convictions that underlie the most modern and snappy of productions are simpleminded or oldfashioned. But dig for them and you will find them. A play can't be written without them—or, at least, it can't be a success—because no audience is satisfied with a play which doesn't take an attitude toward the world. (20-21)

The best atmosphere for the practice of playwriting is a stable society amid a stable group of nations, but the confused and unstable condition of our present-day society make it even more necessary for the playwright to have an attitude toward the world around him. Anderson emphasized that "those who have kept going as writers within it have done so because they could cling to inner beliefs not easily destroyed by exterior storm. Or because they believed in nothing and could stimulate whatever belief happened to be popular"(20-21).

It is Anderson's further belief that the theatre is "the central artistic symbol of the struggle of good and evil within men"(33). The theatre offers us criteria for judging what is evil and what is good in man, for as Anderson analogizes, if a man such as Adolf Hitler had been set upon the stage, even in Germany, the audience would have responded with loathing (34). The reason for this is that

> the audiences, sitting in our theatres, make these rules and, in setting them, define the purposes and belief of homo sapiens. There is no comparable test that I know of for what is good in the human soul, what is most likely to lead to that

distant and secret destination which the race has chosen for
itself and will somehow find. (35)

Anderson was very cognizant of his audience's moralistic demands. Whether
he arrived at this point of view from his long association with the theatre
audience or from his own conviction is unknown. But that his writings
reflected this concept there can be no doubt. He was such a writer at the time
this essay was written in 1941.

Anderson wrote a few other essays after "Off Broadway," but with
the exception of one comment in an essay on George Bernard Shaw, called
"St. Bernard," written in 1946, there is nothing new concerning his rules of
playwriting. This one comment has to do with the difference between comedy
and tragedy and explains why the majority of Anderson's plays have to do with
tragic themes, for it is indicative of his belief that the ultimate purpose of
theatre is the exaltation of the spirit of man. Anderson says,

> The difference between comedy and tragedy seems to be
> this—the writer of comedy assumes that something can be
> done immediately to save men from themselves, and the
> writer of tragedy knows that there is no immediate way out.
> He knows that the burning questions of reform are all old,
> that men have sought the answers since the morning of
> history, and that the answers will not be found in his time,
> that nothing final will come of anything he does or says. (*Off
> Broadway* 15-16)

This point of view seems rather pessimistic on the surface as far as a tragic
writer is concerned, but coupled with Anderson's statement that he hopes
mankind will eventually raise itself toward the ultimate goal as has been done
in the past, it assumes a more hopeful perspective. This, then, is one more guide
that a playwright might follow in writing: that the essential difference between
a work that is comic in nature and a work that is tragic is in the attitude of the
playwright toward man as he is and man when he will become better. This rule
or guide does not seem to be meant to restrict a writer to only one form, tragedy
or comedy, but rather it seems to apply to the attitude of the playwright in each
play.

From the discussion of the various essays on theatre that Anderson
wrote, several rules or guides have been mentioned or pointed out. It has also
been determined that these rules or guides were developed over a period of
time as Anderson wrote his plays. As Anderson admits, "I developed a theory
which still looks cogent to me—that a playwright's first success was always
largely accidental. After that he could analyze what he had done, and begin to
develop an intuition that would take him through the maze of difficulties and
dangers his action and dialogue must read"(24). That Anderson did look back

on his successes and on his failures and profited by them is apparent in his long career. In response to a questionnaire published in *The Saturday Review* in September, 1955, Anderson advised someone who wanted to make playwriting his profession, "If you want to write, write, but do not talk about it. Be insanely certain of yourself and sanely critical of all you do"(Hewes 18).

The progressive stages in the chronological development of Anderson's rules cannot be emphasized enough, for they reflect a great deal about his artistic conscience. There are strong indications that Anderson had at least partially formulated some of the rules by the time he wrote *Elizabeth the Queen* in 1930: (1) in this play he followed, at least in part, most of the rules that he later recorded in his essays; and (2) after the failure of *White Desert*, Anderson did not return to poetry as a medium for a play until he had discovered that poetic drama had never been successful when written about one's own time and place, which suggests that he was seeking for the best methods to construct his plays. It is apparent that, by the time Anderson wrote *Winterset* in 1935, he had, at least in his mind, all of his rules, for *Winterset* is the first play that follows all of the rules as he recorded them beginning in 1935. Therefore, it is safe to say that during the first 11 years Anderson spent writing for the theatre, he was learning his craft. During the next 12 years, after he had his rules fairly well in mind, he wrote about his craft, probably to save others the difficulties he had experienced in his early search for the best methods to use in writing for the theatre.

The basic disciplines which have guided this study of the chronological development of Anderson's rules are two: (1) it is reasonably safe to assume that he had firmly set a particular rule if he used it in two consecutive plays; and (2) if Anderson disregarded a particular rule experimenting with the rule, for reasons which will probably never be known, he deliberately broke it or chose to ignore it. In the examination of the uses that Anderson made of these rules I have divided them as they seem to group themselves logically into three areas: (I) the playwright's purpose and aim in writing the play, (II) the structure of the play, and (III) the leading character of the play. With this division in mind, the plays will be examined as to how the rules were used or if they were used or altered in any way. Each rule must be considered in turn and discussion of the play or plays and the appearance and/or use(s) of the rules in each case.

I. The Playwright's Purpose and Aim in Writing the Play:

> 1. The aim of the playwright is to recapture a vision for the stage and that vision must be a compromise between what is of immediate concern and interest to the playgoer and that which the playwright has that he wishes to put into words.

71

It was approximately 1933 before Anderson fully realized this rule. Up until that time he had written several plays, some of which were quite successful, but he had not had two successful plays in a row. The year 1933 saw two of his plays appear and succeed on Broadway: *Both Your Houses*, followed by *Mary of Scotland*. This double success would seem to indicate that Anderson had realized that the playwright must compromise in selection and treatment of a particular vision that is written as a play. Before this time several of the plays had obviously been written without much thought given to audience attitude toward a topic or a subject. Notable in this regard are *Gods of the Lightning* and *Gypsy*.

> 2. The choice of vision and the treatment of that vision must be deliberately constructed for a desired end, for a purely chance achievement is not an artistic one.

This rule seems to be one that Anderson followed throughout most of his career. It is only in the later plays that one feels that Anderson had forgotten many of his own rules. A careful reader is able to see in Anderson's early career his progress as he writes each play. The play that seems to be most slipshod in its construction is *The Golden Six*, Anderson's last produced play. Even *What Price Glory*, the first successful play, seems to have more careful construction than does *The Golden Six*. Therefore, it is apparent that in the majority of his works Anderson followed the rules as he discovered them, or lacking them followed his intuition.

> 3. It is not the primary purpose or aim of poetry (or the theatre) to attempt to reorganize the scientific or practical world of men; it may be attempted but is not its primary aim.

Two of Anderson's plays ignored this rule, *Gods of the Lightning* and *Both Your Houses*, and therefore one can assume that he felt, if he did not fully realize all during his years in the theatre, that the theatre was not the place for pursuing such a reorganization.

> 4. The greatest achievement of man is poetic tragedy and, therefore, poetry is the best medium for the stage.

The fact that Anderson did not write all of his plays in verse does not mean that he did not believe in this rule; it merely indicates that he chose not to follow it all the time.

> 5. In essence our drama must follow the pattern laid down by the Greeks in the core of meaning it has for the audience.

Beginning with the plays written in the 1930s, Anderson followed this rule. He followed it with particular care beginning in 1933 with *Mary of Scotland*. Prior to that time the leading characters were, for the most part, admirable people who acted in ways that show them to be better than they thought themselves to be, but a few were not. After that play and continuing until Anderson's dramatization of *The Bad Seed*, the characters in one fashion or another follow this rule closely.

6. The audience goes to the theatre to reaffirm its faith in itself and in mankind and, therefore, the play must follow this concept.

This rule seems to have been discovered and followed about the same time as those just mentioned.

7. The theatre is a type of religious institution dedicated to the exaltation of the spirit of man.

This is especially seen in the plays that attempt to lift man through the exalting influence of verse. Even the prose plays after 1933 take on this task of attempting to exalt the spirit of mankind. The exceptions seem to be *The Bad Seed* (a dramatization of a novel) and *The Golden Six*.

8. Excellence on the stage is always moral excellence.

It seems that Anderson realized this rule after the failure of *Gypsy* in 1929. After the play, his leading characters are moral people or are attempting to become moral after falling from a position of excellence. Anderson followed this rule, with what some might consider the possible exception of *Truckline Cafe* until *The Bad Seed* and *The Golden Six*.

9. The moral atmosphere of a play must be healthy.

This rule too seems to have been followed closely beginning with *Elizabeth the Queen* in 1930. Up until that time Anderson's plays did not seem to take any particular attitude toward a moral or an immoral atmosphere.

10. The theatre offers us criteria for judging what is evil and what is good in a man.

Again, beginning with *Elizabeth the Queen*, Anderson followed this rule in the majority of his plays. Prior to that time the characters had been shown in a restricted light and, therefore, the audience could not get a clear view of them and of their actions. Exceptions to this rule after 1930 are *Both Your Houses* and *The Golden Six.*

II. The Structure of the Play

> 1. The vision of the playwright that is to be recaptured for the stage must be checked carefully according to whatever intuition or rules the playwright has before it can become a successful play.

This rule Anderson seems to have recognized early in his playwriting career, for from the time of *First Flight* and *The Buccaneer* until *The Golden Six,* the plays follow most of the rules that he seems to have discovered.

> 2. Within this vision there must be central scene or crisis wherein the leading character or hero makes a discovery that affects his thought, his action, and his emotions so greatly that his entire direction in the play is altered.

Anderson apparently realized by the end of the 1920s that a play should have a scene of crisis, but he did not make this scene central to the action of the play until *Winterset* in 1935. After that time, in each play there is such a scene of crisis until his last play, *The Golden Six,* where the scene is not central to the play although it is in evidence.

> 3. This discovery must come near the end of either the second or third act, depending on whether the play has three or five acts. In a two act play it should be approximately one-third of the way into act two.

Winterset is again the first play to play this discovery scene in the position described by Anderson. Prior to this play, the discovery scene took play in the last act and usually in the final moments of the play.

> 4. The end result of this discovery is that in a tragedy the leading character suffers death as a result of his attempt to change or to correct a fault or error in himself while in a serious play the hero goes through a lesser ordeal, but the pattern remains the same.

This rule Anderson began to use in *Elizabeth the Queen* in 1930 and continued to use it in the majority of plays he wrote from that time on, with variations. In a few plays the characters suffer as a result of errors not their own. This is particularly true of *The Eve of St. Mark* and *Barefoot in Athens.*

5. Comedy differs from tragedy in that it presents a happier scene and does not end in death for the leading character.

Throughout his playwriting career Anderson followed this rule insofar as no leading character is allowed to die in a play that is principally comic in nature. In the 1920s *First Flight, The Buccaneer, Saturday's Children*, and *Outside Looking In* are certainly not tragic in intent, but all have certain tragic overtones. Beginning in 1930, the plays display a more clearcut distinction in that the plays that are comic in nature do present a majority of happy scenes. Therefore, it seems that Anderson wanted to keep his comedies and his tragedies more separate than he had done before 1930 and the beginning of his work in poetic drama, for which he is best known.

6. The essential difference between a work that is comic in nature and a work that is tragic is in the attitude of the playwright toward mankind and mankind when we will become better.

Here once again Anderson seems to have fully accepted this rule about the time he wrote *Elizabeth the Queen*. He followed this rule particularly in the plays written in verse, for there the plays take an attitude that a person will become better but will not improve overnight and may, in time, be helped by something the playwright has said. The prose plays seem to expect mankind to improve more directly by what is seen on the stage.

7. The play must deal with the inner life. External events are only symbolic of the struggle within.

In the plays that he wrote himself, Anderson followed this rule throughout the entire series with the exception of *The Golden Six*. It seems probable that in his own work Anderson followed this rule intuitively until the early 1930s. After that time it seems that he realized the importance of this rule and incorporated it into the rules he used consciously.

8. The story must be conflict between good and evil within a single person.

Again after 1930 Anderson followed this rule consistently with very few exceptions until his last play, *The Golden Six*. This was done with variations depending upon the makeup of the leading character. If the leading character was drawn as being unaware or perhaps naive, this was the evil that caused the conflict, and if he was selfish or self-centered, this was the cause of the conflict.

9. The playwright must have something to say and must take
an attitude toward the world in which he lives.

Without exception Anderson followed this rule throughout the plays
written after *First Flight* and *The Buccaneer* in 1925. After these two plays,
two rather disastrous failures, Anderson seems to have fully realized this rule
and followed it even to a certain extent in *The Golden Six*. *The Bad Seed* does
not follow this rule, but it is a dramatization and, therefore, not wholly
Anderson's work.

10. A play is not expected to make ethical discoveries but it
is expected to share a common denominator of belief with
its audience.

With few exceptions Anderson followed this rule all during his career
as a playwright. In the 1920s the major exception seems to have been *Gypsy,*
and the other major exception seems to be *Truckline Cafe* in 1946. From this
it would seem probable that Anderson fully realized this rule at approximately
the time he wrote *Elizabeth the Queen* in 1930 and only misjudged his audience
or ignored the rule in 1946.

III. The Leading Character of the Play

1. The leading character cannot be a perfect person; he or
she must have some variation of what Aristotle called the
tragic fault, for he or she must emerge a better person at the
end of the play than at the beginning.

The only leading character in any of Anderson's plays who appears
not be need a change is Socrates in *Barefoot in Athens*. All of the others are
drawn as being far from perfect, or at least naive or unknowing. This much of
the rule Anderson apparently realized from the beginning of his career. The
rest of the rule, that the character must emerge a better person at the conclusion
than at the beginning, is not completely followed until 1935, in *Winterset*. This
is the time when Anderson apparently fully recognized this rule.

2. From the point of view of the playwright the essence of tragedy or
of drama is the spiritual awakening or regeneration of the hero.

To an extent Anderson used this rule beginning with *Elizabeth the
Queen* in 1930, insofar as each leading character does undergo some degree
of awakening. However, *Winterset* is the first play to place this awakening
early enough in the course of the play to allow the character sufficient time to

undergo a major change. So it would seem that 1935 should also be cited as the time of realization for this rule.

3. The protagonist must represent the forces of good and must win, if evil must accept the good and know defeat.

The clear beginning of the use of this rule appears in 1930. The plays that were wholly Anderson's before this time do not indicate a clear usage of it. After 1930, *Truckline Cafe and The Golden Six* are the only plays that do not show with clarity good triumphing over evil.

4. The protagonist must be an exceptional person, or must epitomize exceptional qualities.

The single exception to this rule seems to be *Truckline Cafe*, but even here Anderson followed this rule to the extent that Anne, the leading character, shows the need of certain exceptional qualities by falling short of them.

5. There are certain qualities which an audience admires on the stage: in a man, positive character and strength of conviction; in a woman, fidelity and passionate faith; and there are other qualities an audience always dislikes on the stage: in a man, cowardice and refusal to fight for a belief; in a woman, any inclination toward the Cressid.

After the failure of *Gypsy*, whose leading character does not follow this rule, Anderson seems to have realized the necessity of this guide, for he followed it faithfully in all of the plays that came thereafter. Even Anne in *Truckline Cafe*, who had been unfaithful previously, is shown as faithful during the course of the play and is determined, apparently, to remain so. Therefore, one can safely assume that Anderson followed this guide from 1929 onward.

Throughout the examination of the plays it became apparent that two notions which may be regarded as rules emerge which Anderson neither included nor discussed. The first of these appears in the play *Gods of the Lightning*. In this play two of the leading characters do not even appear in the third and final act, and the majority of the action of this third act is carried on by minor characters. This technique does not occur in any other play examined for this study. Therefore, it would seem to be a rule that the leading character or characters must carry the burden of the action throughout the course of the play; if not, the play is weakened.

The second item that might be considered an additional rule may be seen in connection with *Storm Operation*. In this play the exposition did not sufficiently inform the audience about the leading characters for the audience to become interested in them. These people seemed, therefore, to exist only in the play and did not become real or identifiable to the audience. The rule could, therefore, be that the exposition of a play must include enough about the backgrounds or previous lives of the leading characters so that the audience might identify with these characters and impart to them a feeling of reality. These omissions from these particular plays seem to have been, at least partially, responsible for weakening the dramatic structure. And, therefore, they could be regarded as further guides or rules that Anderson used but did not articulate as such.

From the examination of Anderson plays in light of his rules or guides, it seems fairly conclusive that those rules carried some validity for him and his plays, for when the rules were followed with imagination, but not slavishly, the majority of the time that play was successful at least commercially. And when in the later years of his dramatic endeavors Anderson ignored a substantial number of these rules, those plays were not successful commercially.

Works Cited

Anderson, Maxwell. "By Way of Preface: The Theater as Religion." *New York Times*, 26 Oct. 1941, sec. 9: 1-3.

———. *The Essence of Tragedy and Other Footnotes and Papers*. Washington, DC: Anderson House, 1939.

———. *Off Broadway: Essays about the Theater*. New York: Sloan, 1947.

Childs, Herbert Ellsworth. "Playgoer's Playwright: Maxwell Anderson." *The English Journal* 27 (June 1938): 482.

Clark, Barrett H. *Maxwell Anderson: The Man and His Plays*. New York: French, 1933.

Halline, Allen G. "Maxwell Anderson's Dramatic Theory." *American Literature* 16 (May 1944): 63-64.

Hewes, Henry. "American Playwrights Self-Appraised." *Saturday Review* 38 (Sept. 1955): 18.

Maxwell Anderson's Skepticism

and the Making of His Plays

by Perry D. Luckett,
U.S. Air Force Academy

The most divisive issue in criticism on Maxwell Anderson concerns his moral philosophy. One group of critics sees a consistent romantic idealism in Anderson's work after 1929, especially including the essays in *The Essence of Tragedy* and *Off Broadway*. They take to heart Anderson's statements that the dramatist must be an interpreter of the racial dream and an exhibitor of the exaltation of mankind, and they apply these statements uniformly to every play, assuming the protagonist of each is an example of this exaltation (Foster 87-100; Weinman 60- 63).

But others see a dominant pessimism in Anderson's thought. Harold Watts, for example, believes that Anderson allows the negative forces of the external world to wear away the ideals and resolve of the hero until he is killed or takes his own life. Thus, Anderson appears to explore hopefully but ends up facing a stone wall (222-23). Similarly, Kathleen McNiven calls Anderson's heroes reflections of the sad futility and despair of the author's thinking (118-19). This sharp division of critical opinion is perplexing to the reader of Anderson's plays, and it calls for resolution.

An examination of Anderson's full career reveals that his world view was skeptical rather than either idealistic or pessimistic. He believed not in dogmatic and predetermined philosophies but in freedom of inquiry and devotion to the methods of research and examination, in order to discover always fallible expressions of truth. He said in a 1945 letter to Louis Kronenberger that "a play cannot exist without some kind of affirmation" and that "if a dramatist has no faith he cannot fashion a play" (Avery, *Dramatist* 203). But he also admitted that "a man would be a fool who was certain that his vision of current events was the only right one, who believed that he had come upon the secret of the universe, or thought he had penetrated, for certain, to the basis of things in literature or anywhere else" (Anderson, *Off Broadway* 20). Although every person must form at least fragmentary convictions to function as a human being, mankind exists in

> a world in which there are no final answers, in which every life, every nation, and every work of art must be judged and rejudged in successive years or generations as long as its influence endures, in which no professed solution of any problem—whether in the field of Socrates and Jesus or that of Newton and Einstein, or that of Aeschylus and Shakespeare—will endure forever. (*Off Broadway* 3)

Thus, to Anderson's way of thinking, skeptical examination of experience and willingness to modulate one's opinions when right and necessary are the touchstones of personal development.

Anderson's analyses of traditional and modern poetry are the clearest early examples of this mode of thinking. For example, in a 1919 letter to *The Dial* titled "One Future for American Poetry," Anderson divided English poetry into major and minor streams. The major strain, marked by "sensuous imagery, the purple patch, incense-breathing melody," and a seeking after the "beautiful, preeminently receptive, and emotional," had dominated English poetry from Spenser, through the Romantics and Victorians, to such "moderns" as Masefield and Noyes. Those outside the tradition strove for "intellectually stimulating analysis and gleeful, ironical portraiture," and their appeal was based upon "detached and philosophic observation of the human comedy." Chaucer, Browning, Byron, and Burns at his best were among these poets who "loved the truth and its ironies, and an active intellect, more than the singing robes"(568).

Although Anderson recognized that the past glories of English poetry were largely part of the mainstream, he said that contemporary civilization was too clear-eyed to appreciate the beautiful illusion it had provided. A professed admirer of Keats, he nevertheless admitted that an attempt to imitate Keats in 1919 was "as futile and shallow as the piano reveries of ten years before" and that those who attempted to prettify modern life or to reproduce beauty in mood and speech were doomed to accusations of insincerity and to an impermanent reward. He viewed America's most distinctively national verse as "lesser attempts in the Chaucerian tradition." And he thought the future might lie with "those who are able to look at modern things in modern daylight, and who are willing to report them without throwing about them any glamour of age, distance, or exotic custom" (569). In 1919, he thought of E. A. Robinson as a pioneer in giving voice to these modern things, and thought that with the work of Robert Frost, American culture and values had found a potential medium of expression.

Two years later, Anderson had revised his theories somewhat to allow for what he called a "greater surcharge of emotion" in modern poetry. Through careful reading, he had discovered Robinson's "portraiture" and Frost's "cunning realism" to be more surface technique than truly philosophical observation ("On Modern Poetry" 112). But he continued to denigrate outworn creeds and methods. He saw imagism, for example, as one of several trends toward exteriors in poetry—a documentation of passing lights and shadows, of colors and forms. He appreciated Amy Lowell's knowledge of drawing and color, which made her a master of observation almost unmatched in English poetry, but thought of her finally as a worker in "synthetic chemistry, imitating life with skill but never creating, never recreating" and therefore, a "great craftsman without anything to say" ("A Prejudiced Word" 18). Because Anderson believed that "poetry seems not to endure at all unless it contains ideas of one sort or another," he demanded depth and sincerity of intellectual content for greatness in art.

To complicate matters further, Anderson made statements at this very same time that would appear to contradict his intellectual emphasis. He announced in *Measure* that many contemporary poems represented a "striving away from the ear and the emotions toward the eye and the intellect" and were therefore "efforts toward another ideal" than his own. He went on to conclude that they "fit with the tradition of Chaucer and Burns as opposed to the tradition of Shakespeare and Keats," identified himself with the latter tradition, and called for the "impassioned utterance that endures" as essential to great literature ("Thunder" 23-24). He said there were practically no readers looking for what it is the great mission of poetry to give—exaltation—because Americans were ashamed of emotions and commitments.

This visionary, this harkener after primitive emotions, appears to be an entirely different Anderson from the man who debunked outworn creeds, disbelieved any theory of human improvement not proved by stringent analysis and practical experience, and disallowed inspiration and beauty from the definition of poetry. But it is in fact another, and a lasting, part of the same complex man. His divergent approaches aren't simply a chronological progression toward belief or exaltation. Anderson was "inconsistent" in his comments because he was not a certain kind of critic going through a certain phase or taking a certain attitude toward various schools of verse. Rather, Anderson's appreciation of poetry reflected the many facets of his own mind and depended on a complex, skeptical examination of the evidence at hand. Like Walt Whitman, Anderson contained multitudes, and he, like Emerson, clearly believed that a foolish consistency *is* the hobgoblin of little minds.

For Anderson, the writing of plays was a manifestation of the same process. He said in a letter to S. N. Behrman, dated December 6, 1940, that "there would be no excuse for literary effort if human nature could be reduced to a formula. Literature is a continual reexamination of humanity—its status, motives, failings and ideals—and if it were made according to any set of rules it would come out constantly with the same result" (Avery, *Dramatist* 106). He believed that the playwright works in the same way as others do in their daily lives—through examination and choice: "A play is almost always, probably, an attempt to recapture a vision for the stage. But when you are working in the theater. . .you must make a choice among visions, and you must check your chosen vision carefully before assuming that it will make a play" (*Off Broadway* 57).

During the earlier part of his playwriting career, Anderson chose to admire the exalted emotion of "poetic" plays, such as those of Synge, O'Casey, or Yeats, as opposed to the "realistic" theatre of George Bernard Shaw. His own work passed through a number of attempts at exaltation in historical and verse drama, and the American theatre is richer for them. But the truly skeptical underpinnings of his thought are reflected in his later opinion of Shaw. In 1946, on the occasion of Shaw's ninetieth birthday, Anderson frankly confessed that he had changed his mind about Shaw, and now set him "at the head of all modern playwrights." Although he characteristically reserved the right to change his mind again, he believed that Shaw had established his preeminence by "irradiating almost the whole of the century with the unquenchable wildfire of an extraordinary brain." Shaw had "taken up and defended," then "abandoned and destroyed, practically every position" someone could take "in seeking a faith for himself and for mankind"—thus reaching "as far as thought can reach" and taking in "more territory than any other man whose life has been lived in his time" (*Off Broadway* 16-17).

Anderson must have appreciated Shaw as a "soul brother," for even though they often differed in their conclusions, their modes of thought were nearly identical. Throughout his career, Anderson moved both within and between works, from an affirma- tion of ideals, dreams, or moral principles on the one hand to a critical, realistic, and ironic vision on the other. He repeatedly reexamined issues and points of view, and he withheld any final certainty in his conclusions.

An understanding of Anderson's skeptical principles helps clarify the progression of his plays dealing with such themes as love, politics, or justice. For instance, Laurence Avery has shown what he calls a development in the playwright's attitude toward love—from idealistic, ephemeral, "sublimated sex" to quieter, more realistic, and more lasting relationships ("Attitude Toward Love" 243-44). Avery also points to Anderson's increasing acceptance of American democracy in light of external totalitarian threats, ranging from *Both Your Houses* in 1933 to *Knickerbocker Holiday* in 1938 (*"Both Your Houses"* 5-24). One could easily trace similar changes in Anderson's plays on the justice system— from *Gods of the Lightning* in 1928, through *Winterset* in 1935, to *Barefoot in Athens* in 1951. These variations on a theme (almost like jazz variations on a melody) come about because Anderson tests ideas or concepts in the cauldron of actual experience, allowing different resolutions based on the reactions of central characters to the environment of the play itself.

To illustrate Anderson's technique, I'd like to consider his treatment of honor and heroism in three early collaborations with Laurence Stallings— *What Price Glory, First Flight,* and *The Buccaneer.* Although only *What Price Glory* is well known, this series of plays establishes a foundation for the lasting method by which Anderson typically explored an idea in dramatic form, regardless of the public reception of his work.

Anderson stated in 1920 that the peoples of the earth had been engaged "actively and commendably of late in smashing the remnants" of medieval civilization. State religion and patriotism, which Anderson called the "origins of national pride, the storm centres of great enthusiasms," were to be put aside for the significant reason that they had "failed us in practice" ("The Revolution" 425-26). But although Anderson believed that these changes brought about positive social development, he was also aware that they undercut every traditional illusion of the greatness of people and nations, as well as the basis for faith in anything beyond daily existence.

A major source of this disillusionment was America's involvement in World War I, which Anderson saw as a war for business rather than for any sort of honor or glory. In fact, he was convinced that a general cynicism developed out of these far experiences, which led to the puncturing of "the fallacy of heroism" and severely limited the depiction of characters on the stage. Moderns were much too well informed and had too little capacity for credulity to grant even the most important people heroic proportions. As a character in Anderson's unpublished play *"Campaspe"* (1929) says, "There are no heroes nowadays. We've analyzed heroes out of existence. As soon as a man makes a heroic stand, or sacrifices for what he believes, we put our scientific finger on the complex that made him do it. If a man's normal he isn't heroic, and if he's heroic he isn't normal" (24-25). Anderson believed that the theatre audiences of the day reflected this general despair and superciliousness. They were dominated by fatalism, by a reliance on luck rather than logic, and they had "emerged from the war with the generalizing faculties paralyzed and no philosophy" ("New York's Theatre" 18).

This attitude toward the war informs Anderson's first major success on the New York stage, *What Price Glory* (1924), which was written with Laurence Stallings and which attempted to depict the realistic aspects of soldierly life. A major object of debunking in *What Price Glory* is the belief that war is a test of honor and glory, that all soldiers are heroes looking for a way to exercise their patriotism. At best, soldiering fits the company cook's description of it as a trade. At worst, it is an endurance contest against great odds, formed without the consent of the human contestants and granting little promise, save the continuance of one's life. Stallings and Anderson waste no time establishing the real reasons that motivate the fighting. Kiper figured that he would "Join the Marines and see the girls," and Gowdy "had a brainstorm one day and signed on the dotted line" (*Three American Plays* 6). A new lieutenant, Cunningham, has come for relief from his civilian job as a railroad engineer on the Louisiana Midland, a particularly wreck-prone line. Not one of these men sees himself as the champion of a great cause.

The entire second act epitomizes the dirt and horror of a frontal position in disputed territory, as well as the absurdity of their mission. For example, Lt. Aldrich has had his right arm "torn all to hell" while simply running rations down a ravine to resupply the company's platoons. When he is carried into a bunker, he is in an "indescribable mess of dried blood and dirt, which appears black" (58). Lt. Moore's response to Aldrich's wound is the ultimate reply to those who believed the war was a glorious enterprise:

> Oh, God, Dave, but they got you. God, but they got you a
> beauty, the dirty swine. God DAMN them for keeping us up
> in this hellish town. Why can't they send in some more of
> the million men they've got back there and give us a chance?
> Men in my platoon are so hysterical every time I get a
> message from Flagg, they want to know if they're being
> relieved. ...And since six o'clock there's been a wounded
> sniper in the tree by that orchard angle crying "Kamerad!
> Kamerad!" Just like a big crippled whipporwill. What price
> glory now? (59)

Captain Flagg calms Moore until he can get him back to the lines largely because Flagg knows that the men must continue to believe in the resolve of the officers to bolster their own sagging determination. And he commits himself to what some might consider a heroic act—capturing an Alsatian lieutenant—because the general has promised that he would trade a month's relief from the fighting for a German officer in good condition. As he is about to go on what could be a suicide mission, however, a German detail with a lieutenant in charge is captured by accident at their own lines. Thus, just as chance has brought them together to face pain and death, so blind luck, not heroism, takes them temporarily to safety.

Anderson's feeling that codes of honor and heroism had been smashed by the realities of war led him to pursue new standards of personal courage. In early poems, such as "Lucifer" and "Sea-Challenge," he revealed an admiration for certain aspects of the heroic code. And in fact this same attitude influences *What Price Glory*, despite its anti-heroic emphasis. Its soldiers face decimation with resigned courage, fighting simply because they must and willing to do what is necessary to get the task accomplished. This personal stoicism in the face of adversity is most obvious in Captain Flagg's description of himself to new recruits in Act II:

My name is Flagg, gentlemen, and I'm the sinkhole and cesspool of this regiment, frowned on in the Y.M.C.A. huts and sneered at by the divisional Beau Brummels. I am a lousy, good-for-nothing company commander. I corrupt youth and lead little boys astray into the black shadows between the lines of hell, killing more men than any other company commander in the regiment, and drawing all the dirty jobs in the world. I take chocolate soldiers and make dead heroes out of them. (63-64)

Flagg clearly recognizes the responsibilities of his position and adapts to them with a hard-bitten cynicism that gets him through. Even after the hellish experiences of Act II, and although headquarters reneges on its promise of rest and leave for Flagg's men by issuing a general order to return to the front, Flagg says, "No, I'll go. I may be drunk, but I know I'll go. There's something rotten about this profession of arms, some kind of damned religion connected to it that you can't shake. When they tell you to die, you have to do it, even if you're a better man than they are" (88). It was this last decision that left critic Barrett Clark feeling an uplift not unlike what he had experienced when a military band struck up and soldiers marched. This feeling—in direct opposition to the major thrust of the play—is a testimonial to the authors' discovery of a form of heroic courage in an atmosphere totally devoid of traditional values.

Stallings and Anderson also collaborated on two historical plays, *First Flight* and *The Buccaneer,* both produced in 1925. Anderson himself considered *The Buccaneer* inferior in structure and quality to any of his plays of the 1930s (Avery, *Dramatist* 77), and *First Flight* never drew a kind word from him. But these plays are important to Anderson's working out of a problem, and this working out was always to be his central reason for extending a theme through several plays. They may be read as further examinations of the themes of bravery and honor and as extended studies of the fighting man's character, subjects very much a part of the more famous and well-received play.

First Flight opened in New York on September 17, 1925 for only twelve performances. It is the story of young Andrew Jackson's conflict with the local gentry of the Free State of Franklin (now Tennessee) over their incorporation into the new state of North Carolina. Because he is a state lawyer, Jackson faces the wrath of the independent "buck-skins," the would-be aristocrat and Southern "tall-taler," Major Singlefoot, and a grasping country lawyer named George Dozier. These last two stand in line to duel against him as defenders of an artificial code of honor and ruthless individual "justice" and thus represent a soon-to-be outmoded standard of conduct. More specific conflict develops over a spirited girl, Charity, who is promised to George Dozier, sought by a country boy named Lonny Tucker, and enamored of

Jackson. The attitudes of the three men toward her and toward each other help to establish their characters and to define the authors' concept of bravery.

Although the characters of Singlefoot, Dozier, and Jackson are differentiated in the play, they are all essentially hot-headed brawlers. The rules of the duello provide an artificially "civilized" frame for their acts of malice and destruction, much the same way as the rules of war attempt to disguise the mass mayhem and bloody pain of battle. Major Singlefoot displays his quixotic nature during a card game in the local tavern. He slashes the arm of a Hessian ex-soldier who has made the mistake of dealing cards with his elbow too near the Major's face. When Jackson also deals the cards with his elbow in the Major's eye, Singlefoot is immediately incensed, and he threatens to pull his knife on Jackson for this slightest of provocations. A duel is proposed as a more "gentlemanly" resolution. Though Singlefoot gets so drunk at a soiree the night before the duel that he is barely able to see, he insists that Jackson take his turn after his own shot goes well wide of the mark. He would rather be killed for a trifle than see himself "dishonored" by not being fired on in a duel.

These actions by no means make Singlefoot a complete villain. He actually fills the role of one type of American cultural hero—the brash, heavy-drinking, gambling, yarn-spinning, semi-aristocratic individualist who never turns away from a fight. A mixture of Falstaff and Hotspur, Singlefoot is an entertaining and sometimes sympathetic character. Yet, there is no doubt that Stallings and Anderson found his actions ludicrous and his code misguided. At sixty years of age, his pose is a bit foolish. He is an overgrown boy playing with destructive toys. All his thoughts are for the past "glories" of a military career, which he has romanticized beyond recognition, and his naive outlook on the political structure of the state allows him to be manipulated by the more calculating George Dozier.

Dozier is a prototype of Anderson's manipulators of power. He is described as a "country lawyer, spare, lantern-jawed, forceful, and ominous" (*Three American Plays* 93). He is quite willing to use artificial standards of honor to further his own purposes. His intentions, as Hank Peevey says to Jackson, are to "run his own state" and to "end by running Major Singlefoot, too" (120). His relationship to Charity is also governed by power and bogus sanction. Because Charity's father has promised her to him, Dozier thinks of her as his property and assumes that he can simply clear his way to her by scaring or killing off other prospective suitors. When Jackson merely speaks to Charity in the tavern, Dozier is prepared to challenge him, and Charity's growing infatuation with the fiery Jackson soon leads to another duel. Unfortunately for Dozier, the leading light of the Free State of Franklin, Jackson extinguishes him before his quest for power can become a reality.

With such characters as opposition, Jackson might have been portrayed as an innocent hero who kills in self-defense and who otherwise conducts himself with wisdom and prudence. But the authors take a critical view of their young protagonist as well. The most conspicuous part of his retinue when he first enters is "a long black duelling case," containing a pair of ready loaded pistols, and he wastes little time showing that he means to use them (105). He impugns the manners of the local gentry, makes a point of calling their territory "western North Carolina," and at first refuses Major Singlefoot's invitation to play cards with them. When he does sit down to deal, as I've mentioned, he puts his elbow squarely in Singlefoot's eye, even though he has just witnessed the altercation between the Major and the Hessian. The aforementioned duel at dawn ensues.

The rest of Act I and most of Act II maintains Jackson's character as a "red bantam cockerel," ready to fight and defend his position and opinions against all comers. But there are signs of his better qualities as well. He acts because he is convinced that the state of North Carolina is necessary to the protection of the populace. He illustrates that he is not a "hard-case" like Dozier when he tries to apologize to Singlefoot so as to avoid their duel. Then, when forced to fight, he fires in the air rather than taking advantage of his opportunity to kill. His apparently deepening relationship with Charity also "softens" his character. She believes in Act III that he was "scairt a little by Dozier." Jackson admits that the sound of a whippoorwill outside he window scared him "something terrible" when it went by him and that he is scared "Lots o' times. But try to hide it" (164). Jackson goes on to say that before the Revolutionary War he was scared continually from being thrashed by other boys and by the redcoats. All this emphasis on Jackson's principles and fears gives the audience a more sympathetic view of what could otherwise be a shallow character.

However, the last speeches of the play stress Jackson's inability to face a real test of courage: permanent union with Charity and the daily struggle to establish home, family, and a place in common society. By contrast, country boy Lonny Tucker is a less flashy, more solid man, who is willing to fight George Dozier for Charity if that is what he must do to gain her love but who is more properly fashioned "to build a cabin, break the land, sow the soil, and harvest the crop" for her (174). And it is Lonny Tucker who clearly reveals to Charity the basis of Jackson's character:

> I been watching him and studying his ways. He fights because he don't know how a decent body does a thing. He's foxy and gambly and full o' loud words just to dissemble that he's worthless.... Do you know why he puts on his airs and wears his uniform and talks law and duelin'? Because he's a come-on from a patch o' trash, imitatin' the big-wigs from the settlements and thinkin' he's gentry. If he had blood in him he'd know more than to come into a tavern insulting strangers. (174-75)

Charity rejects Lonny's remarks. But Jackson himself reminds her that she knew he was scared and admits that there "was a world o' truth in what that boy said" (177). Although Charity says she loves him anyway and insists that he must stay with her if he loves her, Jackson takes his "first flight":

> JACKSON: I fooled 'em all pretending I was brave. I was going to cheat you last.
> CHARITY: I wouldn't care. I wouldn't care.
> JACKSON: (*who hasn't the nerve to take the girl, and who therefore mouths a moral sentiment as an excuse for running away.*) But I'm at the loose end o' cheatin'. And if I leave ye now, ye'll belong to me always...above me white and shinin' forever. Goodbye, Charity. (178-79)

Thus, *First Flight* examines several active, apparently brave, and artificially honorable men and finds them wanting. Jackson himself fails in a test of compassion, commitment, and moral courage with relation to another human being and thereby undercuts his carefully crafted facade of bravery.

Donald Boughton suggests in his dissertation that this play represents a contrast between new and old world values: "Old world values of honor, class superiority, artificial manners and pomposity are debunked; appearing pale and shallow contrasted with the bold, rugged individualism and primitive purity of the new world's values generally associated with the myths of America" (78-79). But Anderson's treatment is not so simple. The tall tales and rugged individualism of Major Singlefoot are a part of the new world, and they lead to foolish brawling. George Dozier is similar to the Yankee lawyer/trader of Cooper's Littlepage Trilogy or of Irving's *Knickerbocker History of New York*, but he manipulates old and new world values to acquire personal status. Jackson is a self-made man who affects manners for the purpose of personal aggrandizement. All this, too, is part of the tradition of America. In fact, *First Flight* presents a balance of old and new world values—especially concerning honor and courage—points out strengths and limitations in each and leaves the reader with the opportunity to determine what is the proper combination of these values in a civilized society of free individuals.

The Buccaneer, which opened October 2, 1925 and ran for just 20 performances, is a continuation of issues that informed *What Price Glory* and *First Flight*. The major thrust of this story about Henry Morgan, a privateer under the commission of Charles II, is once more a contrast between artificial codes of honor and real bravery and strength of character. The duelling, foppish gallants at the rotten center of Charles's kingdom have done nothing courageous themselves and have bought the titles they bear so proudly. And the commodore of the king's navy is a pompous aristocrat, jealous of Morgan's successes. They form a contrast to the manly, courageous, spirited commoner,

Henry Morgan, who argues by example for an aristocracy of talent and worth rather than one of birth. Perhaps this story of a British buccaneer could reasonably be included in a volume entitled *Three American Plays* because Morgan's character has so much in common with epic "American" figures such as Captain John Smith, whose writings on New England and Virginia emphasized exactly this new kind of aristocracy of merit.

Morgan has many of the simple "heroic" attributes of Jackson, but the authors gave him a more mature character in terms of his relationship to the main love interest, Donna Lisa. He plays the courtier to some extent, as Jackson did with Charity, and he adopts the same self-assured, almost swaggering tone that Jackson had presented as a front to Charity and the other frontier folk. Morgan's proposals to Donna Lisa in Act II make him much the same kind of roving adventurer that Lonny Tucker decried Jackson as being in *First Flight*. Morgan says: "To love most men is domesticity; to love me is an adventure. I offer only arms that are more familiar with tiller and sword than with soft encounters" (*Three American Plays* 227).

But Morgan is different from Jackson in his antagonists and in his development as the play progresses. His chief foes have not the sympathetic qualities of a Major Singlefoot, nor the ominous skill of a George Dozier, not the forthright independence of a buckskin frontiersman or a Lonny Tucker. Morgan is clearly the best man of the play because he emerges as a bold, essentially honest, and truly brave individual in the midst of a supercilious and decaying monarchy.

Morgan also is able to refuse a fight when it is of no consequence to him. He bears the insults of three would-be knights and walks away. Later, he says that he will fight with one of them only if the knight will agree to come with him as his officer—if defeated and unhurt. When the fellow refuses the conditions, Morgan has the good sense and courage to decline his challenge:

> It means nothing to me what you think of me in this woman's town, this lackey's paradise. Judge me by your standards and be damned to them—I've better standards of my own. Must I fight every boy who owns a sword and doesn't like my conversation? I'll fight when I have a cause worth fighting for and an antagonist who's won his spurs. (262)

Morgan's assertion of personal standards of bravery and his refusal to act according to artificial codes of behavior make him a much stronger character than Andrew Jackson in *First Flight* and a better representative of the authors' own views.

In his relationship with Donna Lisa, Morgan also establishes his maturity. As it happens, Donna Lisa is no Charity, no romantic girl of fifteen, except in her independence and strength of character. She is a widow, mature, self-possessed almost to the point of coldness, and singularly unmoved by

Morgan's bad attempts at courtly language or his threats of violence. Yet, her desire for adventure and her real feeling for Morgan later convince her to go away with him, even though she has no promises and no expectations of permanence. And at his trial some six months later, she defends his character against the gallants and accepts his challenge to follow him to the sea. Her free spirit and courage have a great effect on Morgan. Though he admits to King Charles that he tried at first to assail her virtue, he states also that he "made one great mistake" by falling in love with her (250). And when Morgan subsequently returns to the Caribbean and the Spanish Main, he gladly accepts Donna Lisa, not simply as his consort but as "Lady Elizabeth Morgan!" (263) Despite his declared aversion to marriage, he is not afraid of marital commitment to Donna Lisa, and despite his feeling that becoming a knight and a governor of Jamaica will lower his credit with his men, he accepts both from Charles and strikes out boldly to fashion a new destiny for himself.

The Buccaneer is in several ways a less interesting play than First Flight. Its characters are too obviously drawn, and the issues fall into a relatively simple contrast between good and bad systems of government and personal conduct. The courtship of Morgan and Donna Lisa brings to mind George Abbott's claim that inside, Maxwell Anderson "was all romance; he wished to ride a white steed over the mountains and carry off a beautiful maiden as much as the next fellow" (104). Yet, there is some complexity in Morgan's development from soldierly cynicism to commitment. His character appears to combine the best qualities of the Elizabethan hero, qualities such as courage in battle, skill with weapons, and ability to appreciate grace and beauty, with the most appealing aspects of the "American Adam"—high personal standards, disrespect for arbitrary authority, self-reliance, common sense, and sensitivity to the intrinsic value of human beings, without regard to titles and economic status.

Taken as a sequence, the Anderson-Stallings collaborations reflect a definite purpose. The authors showed that traditional values were destroyed by the horror and bloodshed of World War I, for the best reaction that the fighting men of What Price Glory can muster is a dogged stoicism—a kind of paralysis of the moral faculties—to get them through. But First Flight is an attempt to discover values and standards that would reinvest man with a sense of dignity. The authors suggest that the demands of a domestic life are a true test of courage. The man who can face the arduous work and commitment to others that common life requires is superior to the brash and reckless "hero" of tradition. Jackson's incapacity for committing himself to such a life and the tendency of women in the play to deprecate the stolid and unromantic figures who do are evidence of this society's inability to discover heroic values appropriate to a new age. On the other hand, The Buccaneer presents a hero who is not simply "bold, bad, and irresistible to women" (Bailey 124) but strong and independent, capable of establishing and adhering to a personal standard of conduct rather than accepting the hollow codes of others, and capable too of redirecting his destiny through personal choice and commitment rather than allowing the rush of events to obliterate him.

This "trilogy" of American plays thus moves from despair to a limited affirmation—from a belief that all standards had been abolished by the insistent realities of modern experience to a vision of a new measure of personal courage with which to face them. Individual standards may vary. Indeed, the rest of Anderson's plays illustrate the complexity and diversity of these personal choices. But the process reflected in these three plays is vital to every person who desires to rise above mere existence, and it is the essence of Maxwell Anderson's approach to life.

Anderson's use of extant verse forms, his allusions to Shakespeare, Biblical scripture, and Victorian literature, and his penchant for historical drama have generally led readers to consider him a "traditionalist in a theatre of change" (Taylor 57). Anderson himself added to this view in some of his essays published during the 1930s and 1940s. His insistence on the moral value of the past world's great literature and on the theater as a "communal service" gave his statements an appearance of far greater certainty than actually existed in his own mind.

In fact, his vision was never static, for he felt that a constant questioning of experience was absolutely vital to human life. His major purpose for writing was to present the most universal tensions of life in a modern universe and to present them in universal terms, for only by such attention to intellectual issues could he hope to discover meaning in what appeared, and still appears, to be random movement through space. A careful study of his poetry and essays, as well as of his dramas, shows that his answers were often uncertain and that he seldom resolved an issue to his complete satisfaction. Yet, his very struggle against debilitating forces is a vital reflection of life in the twentieth century. Combined with the versatility, skill, and quality of his art, this struggle is sufficient reason to consider him one of our best modern playwrights.

Works Cited

Abbott, George. *Mister Abbott*. New York: Random, 1963.

Anderson, Maxwell. "Campaspe." Unpublished play, ts., 1929. The Maxwell Anderson Collection. U of Texas, Austin.

___. "New York's Theatre." *Measure* 34 (Dec. 1923): 17-19.

___. "A Note on Modern Poetry." *The New Republic* 27 (1921): 112-13.

___. *Off Broadway: Essays About the Theater*. New York: William Sloane, 1947.

___. "One Future for American Poetry." *The Dial* 66 (1919): 568-69.

___. "A Prejudiced Word on Amy Lowell." *Measure* 6 (Aug. 1921): 17-18.

___. "The Revolution and the Drama." *The Freeman* 14 (1920): 425-26.

___. "Thunder in the Index." *Measure* 1 (Mar. 1921): 23-25.

___. "To Gilmor Brown." 10 Nov. 1938. Letter 68 in Avery, *Dramatist* 77.

___. "To Louis Kronenberger." 21 Nov. 1945. Letter 145 in Avery, *Dramatist* 203.

___. "To S.N. Berhman." 6 Dec. 1940. Letter 94 in Avery, Dramatist 106.

___, and Laurence Stallings. *Three American Plays*. New York: Harcourt, 1926.

Avery, Laurence G., ed. *Dramatist in America: Letters of Maxwell Anderson, 1912-1958*. Chapel Hill: North Carolina UP, 1977.

___. "Maxwell Anderson: A Changing Attitude Toward Love." Modern Drama 10 (1967): 241-48.

___. "Maxwell Anderson and *Both Your Houses*." *North Dakota Quarterly* 38 (Winter 1970): 5-24.

Bailey, Mabel D. *Maxwell Anderson, The Playwright as Prophet*. New York: Abelard, 1957.

Boughton, Donald J., Jr. "The Broadway Plays of Maxwell Anderson." Diss. U of California, Santa Barbara, 1975.

Foster, Edward. "Core of Belief: An Interpretation of the Plays of Maxwell Anderson." *Sewanee Review* 50 (1942): 87- 100.

McNiven, Kathleen E. "Idealism in the Plays of Maxwell Anderson." Thesis. Cornell U, 1943.

Taylor, William E., ed. "Maxwell Anderson: Traditionalist in a Theatre of Change." *Modern American Drama: Essays in Criticism.* Deland, FL: Everett Edwards, 1968. 47-57.

Watts, Harold H. "Maxwell Anderson: The Tragedy of Attrition." *College English* 4 (1943): 220-30.

Weinman, Richard J. "The 'Core of Belief' of Maxwell Anderson and the Structure of His Tragedies." Diss. Indiana U, 1965.

Maxwell Anderson, Lyricist

by John Bush Jones,
Brandeis University

By his own account, when, at the age of twenty-nine, Joshua Logan was invited by Kurt Weill and Maxwell Anderson to direct *Knickerbocker Holiday*, he thought upon first hearing the score that "it wasn't Dick Rodgers, and Max wasn't Larry Hart, but everything about Kurt Weill was talent and enthusiasm. And Max's lyrics were poetic and funny. I knew I wanted to do the show and I told them so" (Logan 129). For Logan, the comparison of Weill and Anderson to Rodgers and Hart was neither random nor arbitrary but rather based on a very personal association with the latter pair. The young director had just completed staging Rodgers and Hart's enormously successful *I Married an Angel*, a musical that would ultimately prove to have a longer run than the project Logan was embarking on with Weill and Anderson.

Still, while Logan's mental assessment of the songs for *Knickerbocker Holiday* was based on personal experience, his observation was very astute and remains useful in a broader way for its tacit implication that the collaboration of Weill and Anderson was somehow different not only from Rodgers and Hart *specifically*, but also generally, as they represent the mainstream of composers and lyricists for the Broadway musical stage of the period, a partial list of whom might include Cole Porter, Irving Berlin, Jerome Kern and Oscar Hammerstein II, and the recently departed George Gershwin and his brother Ira. Indeed, neither *Knickerbocker Holiday* (1938) nor *Lost in the Stars* (1949), the only two Anderson/Weill musicals to be produced on Broadway,[1] can be said to follow in the main traditions of American musical theatre of those decades. The former in many ways harks back to the conventions of nineteenth- and earlier twentieth-century operetta and, especially, the comic operas of Gilbert and Sullivan, while the latter is a somewhat daring, forward-looking, even experimental piece adumbrating later innovations in musical theatre form and style. What is more, the "derivative" nature of *Knickerbocker Holiday* and the "progressive" nature of *Lost in the Stars* is apparent not only in the overall plotting and structure of these two musical shows but also in the kinds of lyrics Anderson wrote for them and in the very functions that the musical numbers in each perform with respect to larger considerations of character, action, ideas, and dramatic or ideological perspectives.

It would appear at first blush that the leap from writing verse plays to song lyrics would have been an easy one for a man like Maxwell Anderson, who was as eloquent in his essayistic defenses of verse as a viable medium for modern drama as he was prolific in his writing of poetic plays. And yet an examination of *Knickerbocker Holiday* and *Lost in the Stars* strongly suggests that Anderson saw songs and other musical sequences as something special, something generally set quite apart from the action of a musical, rather than as embodiments of that action, as would be the dialogue of a non-musical verse drama. This, despite a piece by Jack Gould in the *New York Times* shortly before the opening of *Knickerbocker Holiday*, a piece that purported to describe Anderson's approach to the writing of the play:

> The team of Anderson and Weill broke with precedent from the start. Unhampered by any fealty to musical comedy experience, Mr. Anderson wrote the lyrics for the music just as he came to them in the book. The lyrics are an integral part of the story—no tangents about the moon and croon and love and heaven above—and Mr. Anderson saw no reason for doing the book first and then going back to the songs, as is customary. When Mr. Weill was ready to go to work he found a completed script and wrote the music to fit the words. Both composer and lyricist completed their tasks in about three weeks. (1)

Gould nowhere indicates if his information on Anderson's habits of composition came from an interview with the playwright himself, but even if it did, and even if it is true that he wrote the song lyrics sequentially as places for songs occurred to him in the writing of the dialogue, a reading of *Knickerbocker Holiday* swiftly reveals that while many of the songs are indeed integral to Anderson's expression of his ideas and feelings about American politics and politicians which permeate the play, few if any are truly "an integral part of the story." In fact, virtually all of the songs could be eliminated and the entire story-line of *Knickerbocker Holiday* would remain intact. Also, the reliability of Gould's reportage may be further questioned, since we know that at least one number, the classic "September Song," was written after most of the libretto was complete in order to flesh out the role of Pieter Stuyvesant to make it more attractive to Walter Huston, for whom Weill, Anderson, and Logan were angling for the part (Shivers 174-75).

Anderson's use of songs in *Knickerbocker Holiday* becomes more understandable if we consider his model for the writing of this, his first musical play. Logan was right in noting that Anderson was not looking to the conventions of the popular musical comedy of the day for inspiration but well back beyond them. By his own subtle admission, Anderson's writing of both the book and lyrics of *Knickerbocker Holiday* had as its principal prototype the satiric comic operas of Gilbert and Sullivan, most specifically *The Mikado*.[2] That Anderson was particularly familiar with *and* particularly fond of the Gilbert and Sullivan operas as exemplars of the musical theatre genre is clear from a remark in his letter to Elmer Rice of June 26, 1938: "Weill's music is the best I have ever heard for any musical show, better even than Sullivan's. If the words are only half as good and we have the right actors, we should come off very well" (Avery 74). Not only does this remark demonstrate Anderson's admiration for Gilbert and Sullivan, but it raises further questions about his lyric writing. Is he worried here about how lyrics he has already written will sound in the show, or is he wondering how some yet-to-be-written lyrics will turn out—lyrics, it would appear from the sense of the sentence, that are to be written to melodies already composed by Weill (an unlikely possibility, given Weill's usual habits of musical compositions)?

However Anderson did in fact compose those lyrics, the end product was largely a body of witty, sophisticated, sometimes downright erudite, and occasionally sentimental songs very much in the vein of Gilbert and Sullivan in the elevated level of their diction and the complexity of their syntax and rhymes. And very often these songs function in the ways songs function in Gilbert's formulaic plotting of his libretti. This should come as no surprise, for the mechanics of Anderson's plot of *Knickerbocker Holiday* agree in many particulars with the mechanics of Gilbert's plot for *The Mikado*. Both plays begin with a group of bumbling small-town politicians (Ko-Ko, Pooh-Bah, and Pish-Tush in the town of Titipu; the comic Town Council in old New Amsterdam) deciding they must execute someone, partly to fulfill the letter of a ludicrous law, partly to impress a tyrannical ruler (the Mikado himself in Gilbert, the new Governor Stuyvesant in Anderson) who is to arrive in town that very day. In each case the intended victim is in love with, and loved by, a young woman who is betrothed to one of the play's authority figures. In *The Mikado*, Nanki-Poo's love for Yum- Yum is complicated by her engagement to Ko-Ko, the Lord High Executioner; in *Knickerbocker Holiday*, the rebellious Brom Broeck's love for Tina, daughter of Councilman Tienhoven, is thwarted for a time by her father's arranging her marriage to Stuyvesant himself. As Nanki-Poo (who is really royalty) appears to be "a wandering minstrel. . ./A thing of shreds and patches" and therefore, not a suitable match for the supposedly more highly born Yum-Yum, so too is the rough-and- ready working-class Brom (a type, for Anderson, of the feisty, independent American) not a fit husband for Tina in the eyes of her comfortably rotund bourgeois father. By the end of both *The Mikado* and *Knickerbocker Holiday*, of course, the condemned men are reprieved and the lovers reunited, in each case through a bizarre bit of wholly fallacious but wonderfully comic logic-chopping. Anderson goes so far as to bring in the play's narrator, Washington Irving, as a totally preposterous deus ex machina to confront Stuyvesant directly with the negative view posterity will have of him if he proceeds to execute Brom, prevent the lovers from marrying, and, in general, continue his dictatorial mode of government.[3] And finally, in both musicals there is a happy ending for everyone, with even the villains (who are, indeed, so lovable at bottom that one can never take their villainies too seriously) brought into the comic resolution and general rejoicing of the *finale ultimo*.

With so many particulars of Anderson's plot following the Gilbertian model and his satire centering on governmental tyranny and political corruption as in *The Mikado*, it is hardly remarkable to find that many of the song-lyrics in *Knickerbocker Holiday*, both with respect to their content and placement, follow the musical programming of the typical Gilbert libretto. The opening chorus of Dutch Maidens scrubbing their stoops lets the audience know exactly where and who they are as surely as *H.M.S. Pinafore's* sailors "sail the ocean blue or the lady aesthetes of *Patience* declare themselves to be "twenty love-sick maidens." Roosevelt and the Council and then, later, Stuyvesant and other principal characters have songs upon their entrances detailing aspects of their career and personality, much in the manner of, say, Ko-Ko's "I've got a little list," the Mikado's "My object all sublime," or Sir Joseph Porter's "When I was a lad." In this kind of comic patter song, even Anderson's method is similar to Gilbert's in frequently having the chorus echo the closing lines of the soloist's verses, as

> *Stuyvesant*
> When a military man is at the height of his career
> And marching his battalion off to wars,
> He's fought numerous engagements for his country
> far and near
> In serving his apprenticeship to Mars.
> And he naturally accumulates some decorative
> scars
> In serving his apprenticeship to Mars.

> *Chorus*
> And he naturally accumulates some decorative scars
> In serving his apprenticeship to Mars. (Knickerbocker 93)

Similar too to Gilbertian models are Anderson's love duets for the young couple, a formal wedding processional sung by the chorus (there is one in nearly all the Gilbert and Sullivan operas!), and set-pieces for soloists or small groups to articulate aspects of the play's satire commentary.

What is far more interesting than these similarities, however, are those of Gilbert's uses of musical numbers that Anderson has either chosen to ignore or has simply overlooked in creating lyrics for *Knickerbocker Holiday.* It is, indeed, the virtual absence of two types of musical sequences from the play that makes it possible for the story to exist intact entirely independent of songs. What Anderson failed or deliberately chose not to adopt from his model is Gilbert's use of musical numbers as "sung thought" and, most important, as "musical scenes," both of which functions of singing are not only central to the Gilbert and Sullivan operas, but also—partly because of the widespread influence of Gilbert and Sullivan on the development of the American musical—have become two of the key ingredients in the development and refinement of the modern "integrated musical." Simply put, the integrated musical is a musical play in which all elements of production, including songs and dance numbers, are organic parts of the whole, working toward becoming a coherent dramatic event in which musical and dance numbers are part of a dramatic action and the lyrics to those songs are logical, plausible extensions of the characters' dialogue. While it is generally agreed that the starting-point for the history of composers, lyricists, and librettists deliberately crafting integrated musicals for the Broadway stage was Rodgers and Hammerstein's groundbreaking *Oklahoma!* in 1943, nevertheless Anderson in 1938 still had his beloved Gilbert and Sullivan operas as a prototype for the dramatic function of musical numbers, not to mention a few isolated attempts at integrated musicals on the American stage such as Kern and Hammerstein's *Showboat* (1927) and Gershwin, Gershwin, Kaufman, and Riskind's *Of Thee I Sing* (1931—and also based on the model of Gilbert and Sullivan).

What is meant by "sung thought" is nothing more nor less than the musical theatre equivalent of the Elizabethan dramatic convention of the soliloquy or the operatic convention of the aria, allowing, here through song, the direct revelation of the character's unspoken thoughts and feelings or even (as in, say, Billy Bigelow's song actually titled "Soliloquy" in *Carousel*) the playing out of an inner drama within a single character. The Gilbert and Sullivan operas abound in musical numbers used to reveal a character's inner turmoil—frequently the soprano heroine so expressing her psychological state through such an aria, as in Josephine's "The hours creep on space" in *H.M.S. Pinafore*—but Anderson, for all his Gilbertian borrowings, omits completely this use of song from *Knickerbocker Holiday.* Whether this was by design or not, it is impossible to say.

More telling, and ultimately more damaging to the dramatic consistency of *Knickerbocker Holiday,* is the virtual absence of musical scenes. A musical scene is a single song (such as "Do You Love Me?" in *Fiddler on the Roof*), a grouping of interconnected songs (such as "A Boy Like That" and "I Have a Love" in *West Side Story*), or an extended passage of musical numbers with, perhaps, some intermittent spoken test (such as the first-act finale in *Of Thee I Sing*) that is used to further the plot and/or develop character relationships in exactly the same way that dialogue functions in a non-musical play. Indeed, a well-crafted musical scene often *replaces* dialogue and, because of the compressed nature of poetic song-texts and music, it can frequently move the action along much more swiftly than can conventional dialogue. The Gilbert and Sullivan operas contain excellent models for musical scenes, especially the extended musical scenes that comprise most of their first-act finales, many of which are complete mini-dramas entirely in song, in which a great number of plot complications can be dramatized in a relatively short amount of time. The first-act finale of *The Mikado*, which Anderson obviously knew well, is one of the most tightly constructed dramatic uses of musical sequences in the Gilbert and Sullivan canon, and yet act one of *Knickerbocker Holiday* ends not with a little drama in song but with a brief choral reprise of "All hail the political honeymoon," the song with which Stuyvesant, assisted by the chorus, introduced himself earlier in the act.

What we have then in Anderson's lyrics for *Knickerbocker Holiday* is a case of the playwright borrowing many of the *types* of songs from the Gilbert and Sullivan operas as well as the *placement* of such songs in the context of the dialogue but rarely, if at all, incorporating Gilbert's dramatic *use* of song in forwarding the play's plot and action. Rather, the majority of the songs are descriptive, informational, explanatory, or thematically satiric set-pieces rather than integral parts of the drama. Only a few function to reveal character fully (such as Brom and Tina's declaration of love for one another in "It Never Was You" or Stuyvesant's poignant awareness of his advancing years in "September Song"), and fewer still do anything toward moving the story along. Even those that do, such as Tina's expression of defiance toward her father in "Young People Think About Love," tend merely to restate musically what has already been said in dialogue rather than replace prose conversation with dramatically-charged musical sequences.

It is almost as if Anderson the accomplished verse dramatist, in his first outing as a musical theatre librettist, somehow mistrusted the ability of song-lyrics to carry even isolated moments of a play's plot and action, using song instead almost exclusively for the expression of his own political commentary, satiric jabs, and the occasional revelation of a character's emotional state, as in the show's conventional love songs. And when much of Anderson's lyric writing for *Lost in the Stars* eleven years later is theatrically and imagistically powerful, psychologically probing, and even strikingly innovative in the uses he and Weill found for musical sequences, once again the musical scene—now six years after the Rodgers and Hammerstein revolution and in a decade in which the integrated musical had become the norm on Broadway—is still glaringly conspicuous by its absence.

What is immediately apparent from even a casual acquaintance with *Lost in the Stars* is that this is a different kind of musical, indeed a *deliberately* different kind of musical from the general run of Broadway shows, including those more plausible, more realistic integrated musicals that come to appear with more regularity each season ever since the enormous success of *Oklahoma!* paved the way for a new kind of show that could hardly be classified as "musical comedy." Indeed, Weill and Anderson's innovative *Lost in the Stars* opened on Broadway in the same year as Rodgers and Hammerstein's more conventional *South Pacific*, the latter, interestingly, directed by Weill and Anderson's own director of *Knickerbocker Holiday*, Joshua Logan—both musicals making powerful statements about the need for interracial tolerance, acceptance and brotherhood, though in very different ways.

That Anderson and Weill intended from the start for *Lost in the Stars* to be different by design from the more normative musicals of the day is apparent from the playwright's remark in an acceptance speech for a Brotherhood Award from the National Conference of Christians and Jews that the subject matter of the musical's source, Alan Paton's novel *Cry, the Beloved Country*, "fitted exactly into the scheme for a musical tragedy which Kurt Weill and I had hoped for some years to be able to write" (Avery 300). Moreover, in his letter to Paton himself on March 17, 1949, in which Anderson detailed his plan for adapting the novelist's story of South African racial tensions as they personally touch the lives of a black minister and a white planter, the dramatist declared, "I think it can be as touching and tragic in the theatre as on the printed page" (Avery 222). Clearly, the very notion of a musical tragedy for the New York stage (not, mind you, a full-scale opera on Broadway such as Gershwin's *Porgy and Bess* in 1935 or Weill's own *Street Scene* in 1947 but a tragic musical comprised of both dialogue and song) was a radical departure from the norm in 1949, eight years before Bernstein, Laurents, and Sondheim's *West Side Story* further redefined the possibility for serious musicals in the commercial theatre.

Equally radical as the notion of a tragic musical was Anderson and Weill's original plan for the use of music in *Lost in the Stars*, again as initially explained by Anderson to Paton:

> My first concern would be to keep as much as possible of the dialogue and the story structure, just as they stand. Your effects are both powerful and delicate—and both the power and the delicacy could be lost in the ordinary dramatization. And to keep the plot and the dialogue in the form you gave them would only be possible if a chorus—a sort of Greek chorus—were used to tie together the great number of scenes, and to comment on the action as your comment on the philosophic and descriptive passages. Of course, I should have to put some of that comment into verse, but some of the lyric prose could be lifted out intact and set to music. Kurt Weill, who would make the musical setting, is as enthusiastic about the book and about this dramatic method as I am. (Avery 221-22)

So, at the outset, *Lost in the Stars* was intended to be a play with music, the choral passages serving exclusively as the authorial voice of narration, description, and commentary, while the story itself was to be dramatized strictly through the dialogue of the characters. But the concept changed as the work progressed. Anderson ultimately did make significant alterations in Paton's "dialogue and. . .story structure, just as they stand," even eliminating some key characters and radically changing the novel's ending—this, allegedly with Paton's approval and perhaps even at his suggestion (Avery 230, n. 1), though it is hard to imagine Paton's acceptance of Anderson's replacement of the novel's truly tragic closing with the overly hasty and overly sentimental reconciliation between James Jarvis and Stephen Kumalo that closes the musical.[4] And if Anderson's conception of the script altered during the writing process, so too did his and Weill's vision of the use of music and song in the play. According to Weill's biographer Ronald Sanders, the composer and playwright got down to serious work on what was to become *Lost in the Stars* in December of 1948, and by late February of 1949 "a few individual songs had now made their way into the script alongside the choruses" (377). More were to follow, chiefly at the suggestion of Rouben Mamoulian, the man both Weill and Anderson wanted to direct their new musical. When they played him the score as it then stood in April, 1949, Mamoulian said that he liked what he heard but felt that more musical numbers were needed. "Explaining how he thought the music and the action could be more fully integrated, he even suggested specific places at which songs could be inserted" (Sanders 377). Not surprising observations at all, coming as they did from the director of that breakthrough integrated musical, *Oklahoma!*

Still, even with the addition of more songs for the principal characters, the final version of *Lost in the Stars* bears few resemblances to the mainstream musicals of the 1940s, instead looking forward to more innovative uses of music in the musicals of the decades to follow. And yet, quite mysteriously, and despite Mamoulian's suggestion, Anderson was still not using song to forward the plot and action, a function of music that had become positively commonplace in musicals by 1949. Indeed, a breakdown of the play's seventeen musical numbers reveals that nine are performed by the chorus and its Leader and that only eight are solo pieces for characters in the story itself. Of these, the bawdy "Who'll Buy" is sung by Linda as a nightclub act in her only appearance in the play and, as such, has no relevance whatever to the main considerations of the story's action or characterizations, except perhaps to set up Linda's somewhat sexual banter with Johannes Pafuri and Matthew Kumalo just before these two begin to plan the robbery with their somewhat reluctant accomplice Absalom, Stephen's son. Of the remaining seven songs, two ("Trouble Man" and "Stay Well") belong to Irina, Absalom's lover (and, later, just before his execution, his wife), one ("Big Mole") is sung by Stephen's bastard nephew Alex and a kind of carefree child's game after the pastor takes the boy with him to the relative tranquility of rural Ndotsheni and away from the squalor of Johannesburg, and the remaining four are for Kumalo himself. So, despite the large number of characters in the play, only three who are more or less central to the action are given songs to sing, with even such key figures as Absalom, Stephen's brother John, his wife Grace, and James Jarvis written strictly as dialogue parts, making *Lost in the Stars*, even in Anderson and Weill's final conception, still very much a prose play with music.

Even though Anderson and Weill lifted three of the songs for *Lost in the Stars* from their unproduced musical *Ulysses Africanus*—either intact or with some slight revisions (Sanders 384-85)—these songs, like the others written for Kumalo and Irina, are both potent examples of Anderson's poetry and solid dramatizations of the singers' inner thoughts and conflicts through the medium of music and lyrics. Irina's two laments are superb examples of sung thought, each delineating the tensions between her love and sexual desire for Absalom, on the one hand, and, on the other, her objective awareness that he will come to a bad end. Anderson compresses those tensions with powerful, direct simplicity in the beginning of the verse of "Trouble Man":

> Since you came first to me,
>   Dear one, glad one,
> You bring all the worst to me,
>   Near one, sad one (*Lost* 37)

From there the song builds powerfully to an expression of Irina's loneliness and unfulfilled sexuality of the conclusion of the refrain:

> All day long
>   You don't catch me weeping
> But, oh, God help me,
>   When it comes time for sleeping,
>   When it comes time for sleeping here along! (38)

While it can be argued with some justification that Irina's second-act song, "Stay Well," contains levels of diction and poetic syntactic inversion totally inappropriate from the mouth of a young, semi-literate, South African black woman—such lines as "Go well, though wild the road and far" and "Though into storm your lone bark be driven" (64) sufficing to support that point of view—nevertheless, the song as a whole is another poignant piece of Irina's introspection on her conflicted feelings over Absalom, especially in light of the fact that she is not only pregnant by him but also is aware by now that his execution for murder is almost inevitable:

> If I tell truth to you,
>   My love, my own,

Grief is your gift to me,
  Grief alone,
Wild passion at midnight,
Wild anger at dawn,
Yet when you're absent
I weep you gone. (62)

Both of Irina's songs, incidentally, are presented in the normative manner of sung thought in American musical theatre, with the singer alone on stage performing them in much the same dramatic setting and context as the operatic aria.

The same is true for most of Kumalo's songs and certainly for his most effective ones, in which we see the devout pastor's temporary loss of faith in the musical's title-song at the end of act one and his inner struggle between remaining true to his lifelong preaching on honesty to his son and the pragmatic possibility of encouraging Absalom to commit perjury in order to escape the gallows, articulated in "The Soliloquy" early in act two. Each of these songs develops Kumalo's emotional and intellectual conflicts between religious faith and practical reality, the former through the imagery of mankind "lost out here in the stars" (51) since God has seemingly turned His back on the world, the latter through a direct statement of Kumalo's moral teachings to his son and the fact of the upcoming trial, culminating in the dilemma into which the preacher has been thrust by seemingly irreconcilable opposites:

A man he [Absalom] had given to death,
  Then my words came back to him,
And he said, "I shall do no more evil, tell no
    more untruth;
  I shall keep my father's ways, and remember
    them."
And can I go to him now
  And say, "My son, take care,
Tell no truth in this court, lest it go ill
    with you here;
  Keep to the rules, beware"?
And yet if I say again,
  "It shall not profit a man
If he gain the whole world and lose his own
    soul."
I shall lose Absalom then,
I shall lose Absalom then. (57)

Even in the songs in which Kumalo is not alone but is singing to someone, the lyrics Anderson has written for him are mostly revelations of personal feelings or thoughts. In the very act of describing to his nephew Alex, a boy born to the poverty of Johannesburg's Shanty Town, the simple joys of "A Little Grey House" in the country, one senses that Stephen's graphic descriptions of his home are as much to assuage his own homesickness as anything else. And "Thousands of Miles" (6-7), sung to his wife Grace early in the play, is still mostly Kumalo's personal rumination, as a father, on how unknowable a child's heart and mind can become to his parents over the distance of time and miles, yet ending with the optimistic coda that for all the differences and distances between parents and children, "love leaps out like a leaping spark" (6) over that chasm to unite them in the end. It is these lines that are repeated by the chorus at the play's conclusion to suggest a potential bond between the races, ultimately greater than their differences and the mutual fear and hatred of one another, that *Lost in the Stars* articulates so eloquently, chiefly through its choral passages.

For indeed, despite the addition of songs for some for the principal characters, the originally-conceived choral commentary, narration, and description remain perhaps the most poetically vivid and dramatically effective examples of Anderson's lyric writing (as well as Weill's musical scoring) in the entire play. Too often in the lyrics of the solo numbers in *Lost in the Stars*, as he did with even greater frequency in *Knickerbocker Holiday*, does Anderson get embroiled in erudite thoughts and images, convoluted syntax, and elevated levels of diction, all of which are totally inappropriate to the realistic portrayal of the characters for whom these songs should be plausible extensions of their dialogue, even though the largely comprise expressions of their interior monologues. Conversely, Anderson's writing of most of the choral passages in simpler, more imagistically vivid, and very direct—and this not only when, quite wisely, he lifts some of Paton's lyrical prose almost verbatim form *Cry, the Beloved Country* to become the basis of a song-text.

In his excellent article comparing Anderson's play to Paton's novel from the standpoint of generic distinctions, Myron Matlaw analyzes at length and in detail the nature and function of many of the play's choral passages (270-71), so to do so here would be merely redundant and superfluous. Suffice it to say that Matlaw rightly observes that the chorus and Leader's primary role is to "translate the shifting narrative tone of the novel into quite theatrical terms" and that they are enabled to do this by the very "fluidity and flexibility" of their position in the play as a whole (270). As a nameless and unnamed aggregate of singers, the chorus is free to shift from being distanced, dispassionate observers and describers of the action, to becoming the more subjective voice of "Paton's angry compassions" (27)), and even active participants in the action itself. Matlaw is also correct in observing that the principal effect of all the play's musical passages, and especially those of the choruses, is to "heighten the emotional impact" (276).

Anderson's specific uses of lyrics for the chorus in order to "heighten the emotional impact" are quite skillful indeed. His slightly condensed version of the lyricism of Paton's prose in the novel's first paragraphs as the musical's opening chorus is not merely a descriptive setting of the scene, but further, the contrast of the of the "rich green hills" (2) of the white plantation owners with the valleys inhabited by blacks where "the earth has torn away like flesh" creates an immediately evocative picture of the gulf between the races in South Africa. This image is succinctly reinforced in the lyric to "Train to Johannesburg," through the differences in what the city means to whites and to blacks:

> White man go to Johannesburg,
> He come back, he come back.
> Black man go to Johannesburg,
> Go, go, never come back— (9)

The choral repetitions of "go, go" reinforced by the relentless rhythm of an accelerating locomotive that Weill built into his musical scoring for the piece create a powerful sense of the huge impersonal city swallowing up the endless stream of blacks who pour into Johannesburg in search of employment, never to return to their outlying homelands again.

Similarly, the litany of street names and numbers that comprises "The Search" (17-20) serves both to reveal the mind- boggling confusion of the simple country pastor as he weaves his way through the maze of Johannesburg's slums in search of his son and also functions as a kind of musical collage that effectively collapses the extended time and manifold places of Stephen's search in the novel into a single emotionally packed scene in the play. A similar, and remarkably innovative use of choral song may be seen in the number "Cry, the Beloved Country" (74) and its segue into a reprise of the opening chorus, which, in moving from a lament for the "lost" blacks of south Africa to a repetition of the image of the earth "torn away like flesh" actually effects a scene change from urban Johannesburg to rural Ndotsheni.

One is actually tempted to generalize that the simpler Anderson's lyrics become in *Lost in the Stars,* the more dramatically effective they are. It might be argued that after years of close association with Kurt Weill, both as a working collaborator on produced and unproduced musicals and as a personal friend, Anderson was learning to subordinate some of his tendencies as a poet to use erudite and even archaic diction and syntax, often expressing very complicated thought, to the evocative power of music *as* music. He seems to have learned that simple and direct language, coupled with the emotional range of Weill's music, can be more potent, effectively and dramatically, than more complex, more intellectual, if you will, lyric writing. Anderson's economy of languages is impressive indeed, especially when paired with the haunting dissonances of Weill's score, in such a choral number as "Fear," in which two choruses, one black, the other white, sing after the murder of Arthur Jarvis of "Fear of the few for the many, /Fear of the many for the few!" (46)—succinctly and elegantly expressing the mutual mistrust and apprehension between the two races. Choral sections such as this, "Murder in Parkwold," "The Search," and "Wild Justice," coupling Anderson's most forthright lyrics with Weill's best choral scoring, effectively convey one stage the play's shifting mood and atmosphere as well as provide a point of view and perspective from which to analyze and interpret the events of the story.

And yet, for all the innovative use of musical numbers— especially the choral passages—it must be remarked once again that, just as in *Knickerbocker Holiday,* the appearance of musical scenes to advance the story directly or develop character relationships is nowhere to be found in *Lost in the Stars,* even though by 1949 musical scenes had come to be not merely an accepted but a virtually expected component of American musicals. To explain the absence of musical scenes from even the latter of Anderson and Weill's two produced musicals remains a matter for pure conjecture. It is possible, as suggested earlier, that, anomalous as it seems, Anderson the poet and proponent of verse drama continued to mistrust song lyrics as a medium for carrying a play's action, instead relegating to the dialogue exclusively all the workaday chores of moving the plot along. While making major strides in employing musical sequences to explore characters' psychology and, through the choral numbers, to combine narrative with the immediate communication of the play's varying moods and authorial points of view, Anderson the poet still seemed to deny Anderson the playwright using song as an integral part of the play's story-line, instead seeing songs as something special and set apart from the action. Perhaps, as Matlaw suggests, Anderson viewed song more as part of the affective than the dramatic fabric of the play, its primary function, again, being to "heighten the emotional impact." If that was indeed the case, Anderson the lyricist (at least in *Lost in the Stars*) achieved his goal with eminent success.

If, perhaps, Anderson truly saw song as something isolated from considerations of plot and character delineation, that in itself might help to explain his often elevated language and almost academic expressions of thought, especially in some of the solo pieces, which frequently appear to exist as strikingly independent moments for the verbalization of the playwright's most personal ideas and attitudes rather than for extending characters' actions and feelings into song. Indeed, the anomalies of diction and syntax, especially in the lyrics for *Lost in the Stars,* can almost be overlooked—or perhaps justified or explained—especially when heard set to Weill's elegant music, as a case of song-text and musical score coming together to make a heightened statement beyond the trivial details that are the stuff of dramatic realism. This approach to the musical reaches toward a more universal, even stylized, theatrical form more in the tradition of opera than of conventional drama— laying a foundation that would be built upon by such later innovators for the musical stage as Leonard Bernstein and Stephen Sondheim in their attempts, as Weill and Anderson had attempted, to refine America's one indigenous form of popular theatrical entertainment into a definable and viable art form.

Notes

1. In addition to their two produced musicals, Anderson and Weill also collaborated on *Ulysses Africanus,* based on Harry Stillwell Edwards's novella *Eneas Africanus,* a completed script and score they ultimately abandoned after being unable to secure a producer, and a *Huckleberry Finn* adaptation provisionally titled *Raft on the River,* a project cut short by the death of the composer. Good accounts of these collaborations can be found in Sanders's biography of Weill (see list of Works Cited).

2. In his discussion of *Knickerbocker Holiday,* Sanders (272-282) glances at some of the parallels between this musical and *The Mikado,* though largely from the standpoint of comparing the types of musical numbers composed by Weill and Sullivan for their respective scores.

3. At this moment in the play, Anderson uses the theatrically self-conscious device of having Irving directly and deliberately point to the audience members themselves as examples of the "posterity" that will hold Stuyvesant to account for his actions. This preposterous breaking of the fourth wall to achieve a totally unprepared-for and illogical happy ending may have been influenced by the equally absurd finale of the Weill/Brecht *Threepenny Opera,* but unlike Brecht, Anderson does not appear to be making a parodic statement on the sillier conventions of comic-opera finales but merely using the intrusion of the narrator and the audience for comic effect pure and simple.

4. See Matlaw's article throughout for an excellent summary of Anderson's revisions, excisions, and alterations.

Works Cited

Anderson, Maxwell. *Knickerbocker Holiday.* Washington,DC: Anderson House, 1938.

___ . *Lost in the Stars.* New York: William Sloane, 1950.

Avery, Laurence G., ed. *Dramatist in America: Letters of Maxwell Anderson, 1912-1958.* Chapel Hill: U of North Carolina P, 1977.

Gould, Jack. "Dutch in New York." *New York Times* 25 Sep. 1938, 9:1-2.

Logan, Joshua. *Josh: My Up and Down, In and Out Life.* New York: Delacorte, 1976.

Matlaw, Myron. "Alan Paton's *Cry, the Beloved Country* and Maxwell Anderson's/Kurt Weill's *Lost in the Stars*: A Consideration of Genres." *Arcadia* 10 (1975): 260-72.

Sanders, Ronald. *The Days Grow Short: The Life and Music of Kurt Weill.* New York: Holt, 1980.

Shivers, Alfred S. *The Life of Maxwell Anderson.* New York: Stein and Day, 1983.

The Critical Reception

of Maxwell Anderson's Plays
in Foreign Language Translations
on the European Stage

Ron Engle
University of North Dakota,
Grand Forks

B ertolt Brecht, writing in his working diary while in exile in Finland, entered on 18 November 1940 the observation that the most popular dramatist in Finland as well as in Sweden was "at the moment" Maxwell Anderson.[1] Although this observation made by a playwright who might seem at first to be the antithesis of Anderson poetics strikes one's curiosity, in actuality it is not surprising, indeed, that a playwright popular enough to have a new play produced on Broadway almost every year for three decades should find an audience in foreign languages just as theatre audiences in this country assimilate Ibsen, Chekhov, or Strindberg. Conversely, many leading foreign dramatists have not enjoyed the scope of Anderson's translations and extensive production activity on the English-speaking stage. The number of translations and adaptations of Anderson's works produced in Europe and the breadth of countries and languages involved preclude an exhaustive study at this time. But even a concise examination of the critical reception and reputation of Anderson as a playwright in foreign translation as performed in non- English languages on the stages of Europe is overdue and essential to assess fully his place on the world stage.

The extent of Anderson productions in Europe is somewhat consistent with the rise and fall in popularity of his plays in the United States, and as was the case in the United States, his works attracted theatre artists of high caliber in the most prominent theatres of Europe. A gallery of international names, many familiar to Americans as the leaders in avant-garde movements, are associated with the Anderson productions. In Germany they include Carl Zuckmayer, Erwin Piscator, Fritz Kortner, Hans Albers, Jürgen Fehling, Maria Bard, Marianne Hoppe, Gustav Gründgens, Hans Sahl, Volker Canaris, and Stephan Mettin; in Austria Leon Epp and Friedrich Schreyvogel; in Italy Giorgio Strehler and Guido Salvini; in Poland Leon Schiller and Arnold Szyfman; in Norway Arne Bang Hansen, Inger Hagerups, Knut Hergel, Helen Brinchmann, Henrik Børseth, Ellen Isefiaer, Ada Kramm, and Jack Fjeldstad; and in Sweden Harriet Bosse, Esther Roeck Hansen, Per Lindberg, Lars Hanson, Alf Sjöberg, Inga Tidblad, and Gun Wållgren; and others in France, Switzerland, Finland, and Greece. The production history begins in Berlin with the 1929 Piscator production of *Rivalen (What Price Glory)* and ends with the Städtische Bühnen Münster production of *Knickerbocker Holiday* produced in 1988 as West Germany's celebration of Anderson's 100th birthday.

In 1929, five years after *What Price Glory* opened in New York, Anderson's play was to repeat its artistic success in Berlin, the theatre capital of Germany and the Weimar Republic. The critical attention created by Carl Zuckmayer's adaptation of *What Price Glory* and its subsequent staging by Erwin Piscator paved the way for numerous productions of the play throughout Europe in the same year. Berlin was at its height of theatre activity with three dozen theatres and many more literary cabarets actively supporting every conceivable moral and political ideology. This was Berlin seven months after Brecht and Weill's premiere of *The Threepenny Opera* and one year before Piscator would open the Theater am Nollendorfplatz as his second political theatre.[2]

Zuckmayer had already established a reputation as a major writer. He had worked with Max Reinhardt at the Deutsches Theater and had received the Kleist Prize in 1925 for his comedy *Der fröhliche Weinberg* (*The Merry Vineyard*). In 1928 his play *Katharina Knie* achieved critical acclaim and his most famous play, *The Captain of Köpenick*, a satire of militarism and bureaucracy, would come in 1931. In an interview given a short time after the production of *What Price Glory*, or *Rivalen* (literally "Rivals"—the same title as was given the film version), and only recently published, Zuckmayer explains how the idea of an adaptation of Anderson's play germinated after he viewed the film version of the play in Berlin.

A year and a half ago I saw the film *Rivalen*. I was exceed-
ingly enthusiastic and expressed my pleasure with it accordingly. A German-American with whom I spoke to about the
film said the play was even better. "What play?" I
asked...And so I discovered that over there [America] a play
by the Americans Maxwell Anderson and Laurence Stallings titled *What Price Glory* had played for years with
sensational success. The play, which had served as the basis

for the film, could hardly have been produced in the first years following the war, since at that time no one had the courage to bring former enemies on to the German stage. Because I did not know enough English to understand the slang of American soldiers, I had the play read to me in a literal German translation. I immediately gained the impression that the totality of it *must* be "gripping" because there was a universal community in the experience of all soldiers on the front lines of war.[3]

Zuckmayer was impressed with the "light, dry humor" which gave the play a special "illuminating power" throughout. "I decided at once without even thinking of an adaptation by myself to have the play produced on the German stage." Later it became clear to Zuckmayer that a literal translation would not be suitable because American style, slang, and speech patterns would lose their effectiveness in a direct translation and that to make the speech most effective for German audiences he should "graft on" to the play German characteristics both in language and war experience. He soon realized that he could not remain totally faithful to the details of the original. "I believe, however, that nothing has been changed of its fundamental character."[4]

The production opened on 20 March in the Theater in der Königgrätzer Strasse and initial critical response was highly favorable. Reviews in Berlin newspapers representing a wide range of political views from the extreme right to the extreme left generally praised the production as staged by Erwin Piscator. The outstanding cast included Fritz Kortner as Flagg, Hans Albers as Quirt, and Maria Bard as Charmaine. Piscator was well known in Berlin and it is no surprise that *Die Rote Fahne*, the official newspaper of the Communist Party, praised Piscator as the savior of proletariat theatre, a director who "alone breaks through the desolate and perfumed boredom of bourgeois theatre" and with every new production conquers new ground.[5]

Several critics, who otherwise praised the acting and staging of the production, found the play leaning more towards the glorification of war than a statement of pacifism, or at least they were disappointed that the tone of the production was not sufficiently antiwar. One of the reasons cited for this response resulted from Piscator's use of a conveyor belt in the final scene when the soldiers march arm in arm towards the front line. The effect of the conveyer belt, which Piscator had already used in his production of *The Good Soldier Schweik*, seemed to enhance the glorification of war as the soldiers briskly marched to the front. In *Schweik* the conveyor belt went across the stage from side to side. In *Rivalen* it was positioned from an upstage to a downstage position towards the audience and had the effect of confronting the house. This may have unconsciously intimidated the audience with the image of soldiers marching towards them and the front lines of attack. While the critic of *Die Rote Fahne* found this scene to project soldiers "driven forward as mindless

115

slaughter cattle," other critics reacted to the scene as a glorification of solidarity among professional soldiers. Monty Jacobs of the conservative *Vossische Zeitung* reacted to the production as a glorification of comradery and definitely not a "Tendenzdrama" against war.[6] The play "only defends war kitsch," wrote Max Hochdorf of *Der Abend*, "War is wrapped in marzipan or in dynamite. War beasts are depicted, but they are promised the immortality of the hall of fame."[7] But Heinrich Bachmann of the *Germania* called the play a "true reflection of internal human tragedy." Bachmann recognized the humor in the play and warned "behind the joke lurks in every sentence a dangerous face: the bestial, raging human! Zuckmayer and Piscator have both spared nothing in order to make this clear."[8]

Ernst Heilborn, writing for the *Frankfurter Zeitung und Handelsblatt*, noted that to identify exactly what Zuckmayer did in his adaptation of the play without knowledge of Anderson's original was not possible but also unimportant. "It is possible he added a bit of humor, possibly he heightened the realism of the action. It doesn't matter. Behind him stands Piscator, like a storm in the sky above the preacher preaching from the chancel and pounding on the pulpit.... If you want peace, depict war.... The play flirts with war, the total production says Never-Again-Wage-War."[9]

Although most of the critics praised the acting and staging, they did not agree on the message of the production. The suggestion that the production glorified war disturbed Piscator, and he reacted to this in *The Political Theater*, published in 1929.

Many of its [the production's] ambiguities could have been avoided. Even so, I still do not consider the play to be glorification of war and I never did see it in this light. To regard the soldiers' march on the conveyor belt at the end of the play (to the front line once again) as an apotheosis of absolute devotion to duty can only be the result of a total misinterpretation of my intentions. On the contrary, I wanted this ending to express the hopelessness, the suffocating inevitability of such a march, which is part of my own experience. Besides, there is a battle scene in the play itself in which I attempted to show that I had suddenly developed a taste for the trenches. After all I had done, I could at least have expected my personal credit to be higher, instead of which I received warning calls which managed to turn a mere "sin of omission" into a full-scale lapse in my political convictions.[10]

This, of course, was quite obviously the interpretation that Piscator had intended and since all of the Berlin critics were familiar with Piscator's politics, it is difficult to conceive that these critics were, in fact, not coloring their judgments fully cognizant of Piscator's political viewpoint. Friedrich Düsel in *Westermanns Monatshefte* is openly biased when he writes that Piscator wearing his "leather political agitative blinkers left and right, naturally sees only a war play..." and created on stage a "hullabaloo" accordingly. Düsel calls Piscator a "Stahlhelmpazifist" ("steel helmet pacifist"). [11]

C. Hooper Trask, reporting the success of the Berlin production in the *New York Times*, found it regrettable that Zuckmayer was given top billing over the American authors since "Zuckmayer's work was of the slightest. He has in nowise improved the plot—merely done some cutting and substituted German soldier oaths for the curses of the American Expeditionary Force." [12] Trask may have catered to patriotism in his conclusion since the characters were altered: Flagg is more brutal, in general the characters are more stereotypical and the dialogue is even more crass than the English original. Alfred Kerr of the *Berliner Tageblatt* suggested that Zuckmayer's major contribution may have been the addition of "crass language, profanity and dirty innuendoes." [13] In Zuckmayer's script Charmaine is much more aggressive, flirting, a coquette and it is she who stops the wedding. Lipinsky is a Jewish character in Zuckmayer's script, and there are many other character alterations including the addition of a prologue with off stage voices drilling soldiers in foul language. [14]

Audiences were impressed with Casper Neher's scene design. Neher was well known and had designed the set for Brecht and Weill's *The Threepenny Opera* and had most recently designed for directors Erich Engel and Jürgen Fehling. Erwin Piscator's stage direction was praised by the critics, but as Trask and others observed, even with all his mechanical fantasy the production could not match the power of the film:

> Erwin Piscator, the mechanical playboy of the German theatre, has staged it with what is for him a great deal of scenic reserve. Most of his contributions are good. Two dynamic loud-speakers on either side of the stage transmit to us the atmospheric noises of life behind the lines and with ear-splitting insistence pound out the auditory horrors of war. In the first act the roof of the cottage is transparent, and we see through it an enormous map like a military plan. As the boys go over the top, shadows of close fighting are thrown from behind on a drop covering the upper half of the proscenium. When Flagg and Quirt, followed by the rest of the detachment, set out for the front in the last act, they march on a treadmill toward the footlights with the scenery disappearing toward the back of the stage; a praiseworthy attempt to catch the tragedy of those moving final shots which closed the unforgettable film, but here unsuccessful,

because of technical difficulties which simply could not be overcome.[15]

Rivalen ran from 20 March well into July. It may have even had a longer run if not for the "rivalry" off-stage between the lead actors Fritz Kortner and Hans Albers. Both actors engaged in a brawl in the theatre and Kortner threatened to leave the production. It was reported in the newspapers that the incident was a result of the stage violence in the action of the play on stage continuing off stage.[16]

The critical success of *Rivalen* was to spread throughout Europe in a very short time. Several factors contributed to this: the visibility and influence of Berlin critics, the top notch stars involved, the uneasy political situation in Europe, the desire for an antiwar statement, and finally the reputation of both Piscator and Zuckmayer throughout Europe.

Anderson was to have two plays running simultaneously in Berlin. On 30 April the Schiller Theater announced the German premiere of Anderson's *Zaungäste*. *Outside Looking In* had opened in New York in September of 1925 for 113 performances. The play was based on Jim Tully's novel *Beggars of Life*. James Cagney played Little Red and Charles A. Bickford had the role of Oklahoma Red. In Berlin *Zaungäste* (literally "Visitors on a Fence") was directed by Jürgen Fehling, a director well known for his productions of Kleist, Chekhov, and Hauptmann. One of Germany's most prestigious directors in the 1930s, Fehling was highly regarded for his realistic stagings even during the height of German Expressionism. The realism of Anderson's play seemed to fit Fehling's style, and he was surely familiar with Piscator's production of *Rivalen*. The realism of hobos fighting over the love and honor of a prostitute (who had killed her stepfather for seducing her) set in a box car in North Dakota piqued Fehling's interest. The play opened the day before May Day 1929, which was not the most opportune time for newspaper coverage of theatre events. The Communist Party had threatened a colossal May Day demonstration and most newspapers were busy covering the riots which occurred that day. *Die Rote Fahne*, in fact, was briefly banned from publication for supporting the rioters and was unable to review the opening.

When the reviews did come in several days later, they were not highly favorable. The critics, perhaps not surprisingly, did not associate Anderson with the successful *Rivalen* production still enjoying a long run at the Theater in der Königgrätzer Strasse. Most likely Anderson was overshadowed in their minds with the German names of Zuckmayer and Piscator. Nevertheless, the critical comments are revealing. Arthur Eloesser of the *Vossische Zeitung* ironically declares that America has finally discovered Naturalism. The Russians, like Gorki, started with hobos and vagabonds (*The Lower Depths*) and now America's "young literature has made a rebellious stride forward," he notes, but "what transpires over there as naturalism, is already made too romantic for us merely by the voyage over."[17] This observation is perhaps accurate since even for New Yorkers the "naturalism" of North Dakota may be overly romanticized. In this respect the New York and Berlin critics may have agreed. Eloesser found Anderson's characters not sufficiently "bad" enough to be dramatic and the action of the play too drawn out to sustain interest. "It is not a play, it is three acts," he says, and the open road of the vagabond is "long" indeed. Both Bruno E. Werner of the *Deutsche Allgemeine Zeitung* and Friedrich Düsel, the critic of *Westermanns Monatshefte* also found the play boring and requiring the "patience of Job." In Düsel's commentary, however, the seeds of German nationalism are evident. He laments the fact that foreign plays are all too frequently seen in Berlin. "After 1870 it was the French, after the World War it's the Americans.... There is nothing more stupid and inane than to allow ourselves to be talked into something simply by calling it progress and 'the latest sensation.'" [18] *Zaungäste* played in repertory with Ibsen's *Ghosts* well into June and was also produced at the Kammerspiele in Hamburg later in 1929.

The attention focused on the Anderson Berlin premieres created interest in his more current work. Piscator had considered three versions of the Sacco and Vanzetti affair for production in his new political theatre—Anderson's *Gods of the Lightning* written together with Harold Hickerson, which had opened in October of 1928 in New York for a brief run of 29 performances, and two other plays by Leonhard Frank and Erich Mühsam. The latter's *Sacco und Vanzetti* had been produced by Alexander Granach's November Studio group at the "Theater in der Stadt" in April of 1929. The production was directed by Piscator's protegé Leopold Lindtberg. Apparently Piscator was pleased with the production since he scrapped his intentions to produce a play on that theme. It was reported in the 24 August 1929 issue of *Die Rote Fahne* that Piscator and Mühsam would speak at a memorial performance given on the anniversary of the Sacco and Vanzetti execution.[19] The Deutsches Volkstheater in Vienna premiered Zuckmayer's adaptation of *What Price Glory* on 28 June 1929. Under the direction of Heinz Hilpert, a friend of Zuckmayer and prominent Berlin director, the production did not employ as many special effects as Piscator had used, but apparently enough effects were utilized to stir the generally conservative Vienna critics into complaining about too much business and too many special effects. Ernst Lothar, critic for the *Neue Freie Presse*, found the production to be exciting, moving, and stimulating. In fact everything was fine except the play lacked "ethos." He admits that he was not familiar with the film nor the original script, but the play as produced by the Volkstheater was "a sugar glazed shocker" disguised as ethos. Lothar suggests that the play exploits the current antiwar sentiment and attempts to capitalize on the popularity of recent war literature being published. He also complains that the Volkstheater cut out the scene in the trenches. The absence of this scene may explain in part the reaction to the lack of ethos in the play.[20]

News of the Vienna production spread to Sweden. Stockholm's *Dagens Nyheter* reported the details of the production and noted with pride that Anderson was "svensk" (Swedish).[21] Understandably, Stockholm would seem to be the perfect spot for a production of *What Price Glory*. Indeed, only three months passed before the Swedish premiere took place at the Royal Dramatic Theatre on 5 October 1929. *Ärans fält* (literally "Field of Glory") was directed by Per Lindberg, who had already established himself as a leading avant-garde director. He had produced Yeats and Synge, and his staging of O'Neill's *Strange Interlude* had captivated Stockholm audiences in 1927. The seasoned cast included Sven Bergvall, Lars Hanson, Harriet Bosse, and Anders Hendrickson. *Ärans fält* was generally well received as a "sarcastic" and realistic portrayal of soldiers at the front. The *Dagens Nyheter* critic had some reservations concerning the episodic structure of the play but praised the performances and especially Lindberg's direction. A conveyor belt was used in the final scene and the readers were informed that the production was better staged than Piscator's German version because Lindberg managed to give more shape to the episodic action, especially in the second act. Anders Henrickson's clowish Lipinsky character was praised for its humor and Bosse's Charmaine was especially applauded for her versatility and realism. Bosse, the leading lady of Strindberg female characters (and his wife from 1901-04), had prepared well for the role by traveling to Berlin to see Piscator's production earlier that year.[22]

But Anderson was not new to the Swedish stage. Earlier in January 1929 *Saturday's Children* or *Så'na barn* (literally "Such Children") was produced at the Blanche Theatre by Erik Berglund in a translation by Gustaf Collijn and starred the well known actress Ester Roeck Hansen. The play was referred to as realistic and "honest" comedy, "painful" but honest. Critics were surprised at Anderson's ability to write comedy. The *Dagens Nyheter* critic praised the skill and openness of the sexual conflict without having to hide in Strindberg mystification. Hansen, as Bobby, was praised for her beautiful and truthful performance.[23] Thus, *Saturday's Children* may have been the first foreign translation of an Anderson play staged in Europe. The play's success was repeated in Gothenburg in October in a production directed by Olof Sandborg. In the fall of 1929 *What Price Glory* reached Poland and was produced both in Warsaw and Lodz by two of Poland's leading theatre directors. Arnold Szyfman, founder of the Teatr Polski in Warsaw, produced *Rywali* successfully using the well known actor Junoszy in the role of Captain Flagg.[24] In Lodz Leon Schiller, who had created a scandal with his Warsaw production of *The Threepenny Opera* earlier, produced *Rywali* using projections. Schiller, and probably Szyfman also, based his production on Zuckmayer's German adaptation.[25] Schiller had developed what was referred to as "monumental theatre," making use of non-realistic staging, revolving stages, platforms and projections in his productions of the Polish Romantic playwrights. The techniques were similar to those used by Piscator, and therefore, reports of the Piscator *Rivalen* production would have appealed to him.[26]

Political events in Germany and the rise of National Socialism in the early 1930s would make further productions of Anderson, or any American playwright for that matter, virtually impossible. But in 1935, three years before Hitler's "Anschluss" of Austria, Hermann Roebbeling, director of Vienna's famous Burgtheater, selected Anderson's *Elizabeth the Queen* to represent the United States in a cycle of plays produced as a festival to be called "Voices of Nations in Drama" ("Stimmen der Völker im Drama"). The play was selected as a classic example of drama in the United States. Austrian writer Friedrich Schreyvogel translated the play with the title *Elizabeth und Essex*. The opening was a gala event with diplomatic envoys and special guests in attendance. Henry A. Diez wired a rave review to the *Herald Tribune* following the opening on 8 November. He noted that the plays selected for inclusion in the festival must have "outstanding literary merit and at the same time be characteristic of the spirit of the nation from which they come." He added that

> Maria Eis, the Burg Theater's leading heroine, played the queen admirably, being at her best in Elizabeth's last scene with Essex, ably portrayed by Heinz Woester. Other roles, too, were in good hands, and the audience appreciated the high quality of the work and the perfect way it was produced. The applause was intense and at the end the curtain went up many times.[27]

Elizabeth und Essex was repeated for 13 performances, ending on 2 February 1936.[28]

During the 1939-1940 theatre season two of Anderson's plays premiered in Oslo before the Germans occupied Norway in March of 1940. The first was *Winterset* on 3 October at the National Theatre starring Arne Bang Hansen and Vibeke Falk. Critical reception of *Mot vår* was devastating. It was a "failed performance" but the play, according to one critic at least, did lead one's thoughts towards *Hamlet* and *Romeo and Juliet*. The critic of *Morgenbladet* suggested that the performance did not do justice to the play. Anderson's ideas were like "words with holes" in them. The play was about the search for righteousness, he continued, and the search for truth, but on stage there was "a bloody and violent gangster" play.[29] Another critic felt the play's fantasy-filled plan was "shriveled" to a detective piece with a banal love story.[30] Several months later, however, Anderson would be praised with great enthusiasm in the Norske Teatret production of *High Tor*. The critic of *Morgenbladet* compared the play to *A Midsummer Night's Dream* and *The Tempest* and found the play rich and captivating. Anderson had learned from the Renaissance Master to "allow prose to flow like verse where the voice shall have wings." The critic enjoyed the blend of illusion and imagination in the

121

characters and action of the play.[31] Another critic found the play poetic and humorous, and "one of the most delightful theatre events of the season." The production staged by Danish director Samuel Besekow used the "simple set," designed by Arne Walentin, effectively and captured a fine feeling for the play's style and fantasy.[32]

In the late 1930s and early 1940s there were frequent productions of Anderson's plays both in Finland and Sweden. In Stockholm there were productions of *Masque of Kings* (Mayerlingdramat) in 1938,[33] a very successful *The Eve of St. Mark* (Vi har vår frihet) in 1943,[34] *Winterset* (Grå gryning) in 1940 and *Key Largo* (Morgondagens män) in 1940.[35] In Gothenburg there were frequent productions as well including *Winterset* (Natt över *New York*) in 1937 and *Key Largo* in 1941.[36] In Helsinki *Saturday's Children* (*Lauantailapset*) and *Masque of Kings* (*Furstemasker* at the Svensk Teater, Swedish Theatre) were produced in 1938-39.[37] Anderson was indeed as popular as Brecht had observed.   Perhaps it is no surprise that Anderson was to be introduced to Italian audiences during 1940 and 1941. *Winterset* was produced in 1940 by the Teatro delle Arti in Rome under the direction of A. G. Bragaglia. An early proponent of Futurism in art in his early years, Bragaglia produced plays by O'Neill, O'Casey, Strindberg, Wilder, and many others between 1937 and 1943. No doubt, *Winterset* was an appropriate vehicle that pleased audiences as well as politicians. A change of pace but no less an indictment of capitalism was the 1941 production of *The Star Wagon* (*Viaggio alle stelle*) by the Teatro Eliseo.[38]

Following World War II, Italy would take the lead in producing Anderson with a second production of *Winterset* in 1946 staged by Giorgio Strehler at the Teatro Odeon in Milan. The translation was also published in *Il Dramma* (XXII, 15 January 1946). Strehler in his book *Towards a More Human Theatre* (*Für ein menschlicheres Theater*) writes about his years as a young director when at the age of twenty-four in 1945 he directed O'Neill's trilogy *Mourning Becomes Electra* with only two weeks of rehearsals. The production was successful but Strehler concedes he will never know why. It was the time of Italian realism in the theatre and neo-realism in film he tells us. In his first year of directing after the war, he turned to O'Neill again with *Desire Under the Elms*, to Zola's *Thérèse Raquin*, and finally to Anderson's *Winterset* in 1946.[39]

There were many productions of Anderson plays in the 1940s and 1950s throughout Europe. In France Marcel Achard's translation of *Winterset* was produced in 1946. Achard was a well-known playwright of comedies with a serious undertone.[40] In West Germany there were at least two productions of *Joan of Lorraine* (*Johanna aus Lothringen*) in 1947 and in Hamburg in 1953 with Hilde Krahl as Joan.[41] *Mary of Scotland* (*Maria von Schottland*) and *Saturday's Children* (*Leute wie Du und ich*) were produced in 1947 and two *Knickerbockers* in an early translation performed in Essen and the Hebbel Theater in Berlin in 1948. *Anne of a Thousand Days* (*Anna, Königin für tausend Tage*) was produced in Düsseldorf, directed by Ulrich Erfurth and staring Marianne Hoppe in 1950,[42] and two *Winterset* productions in 1954 and one in 1955 in Essen with Hans Sahl's translation, *Winterwende,* and a third production in Vienna in 1956.[43] Oslo's National Theatre staged both *Key Largo44* and *Masque of Kings45* respectively. In Stockholm *Wingless Victory* (1945) and *Joan of Lorraine* (1948) were successful.[46] In Gothenburg there were frequent productions including *Joan of Lorraine (Flicken från Lothringen)* in 1948, *Knickerbocker Holiday (På Manhattan)* in 1949, *Anne of a Thousand Days (En dag av tusen)* in 1950, and a revival of *Winterset (Storstadsnatt)* in 1955.[47] In 1947 Anderson traveled to Athens and attended the premiere of Theodore Kritas' production of *Joan of Lorraine* with Vasse Manolidou as Joan.[48] In Italy *Joan of Lorraine* was done in Rome in 1949 and *Anne of the Thousand Days (Anna per mille giorni)* was directed by Guido Salvini in 1951 in a beautifully staged production with set and costumes by Giulio Coltellacci.[49]

Anderson's voice was not only heard in theatres, but there were also many radio adaptations. Radio presentations of plays on state subsidized radio stations have always been given careful professional attention in Europe. In 1950 a performance of Anderson and Weill's *Lost in the Stars* was produced and broadcast by the Bayrische Rundfunk in West Germany.[50] But by far the most frequent radio adaptations were produced and broadcast in Sweden. In the 1940s and 1950s at least 17 plays were adapted for radio by leading Swedish writers and directors such as Herbert Grevenius, Einar Malm, Olof Molander, and Karl Ragnar Gierow. They included *Second Overture (Andra uvertyren)*, *Candle in the Wind (Låga för vinden)*, *The Star Wagon (Stjärnvagnen)*, *Lost in the Stars(Vilse bland stjärnorna)*; Anderson's radio play *The Feast of Ortolans (Tramsfågelfesten)* was among those broadcast in 1948.[51]

By the 1960s Anderson productions faded from the stages of Europe. There was one production of *Winterset (Sceneria zimova)* in Warsaw in 1967. But otherwise the only professional productions of Anderson were of *Knickerbocker Holiday* in Oslo in 1960,[52] in Hamburg in 1976,[53] and Münster in 1988. Anderson seemed to wane in popularity with the rise of Arthur Miller, Tennessee Williams, and later Edward Albee. But there was also an increase in experimental theatre activity and a renewed interest in Brecht in the 1960s, along with the seeds of experimental approaches to staging Shakespeare which attracted directors in Europe. Anderson's verse drama, poetic imagery, historical characters, and social commentary have not triggered the vision of postmodern directors. With the exception of West German versions of *Knickerbocker Holiday,* Anderson is rarely produced.[54]

One may find it rather ironic that to see a professional production of Anderson's *Knickerbocker Holiday* in the year of his centennial one had to travel to West Germany. But that is precisely the way it was. The Stadt Theater in Münster (Städtische Bühnen Münster) celebrated Anderson's 100th birthday with a major production of his 1938 Broadway musical *Knickerbocker Holiday*. Certainly the music composed by Kurt Weill was a drawing card. Weill came to the United States in 1933 and met Anderson at a performance of *Winterset* in New York. But Weill was no doubt already familiar with Anderson's work from Piscator's *Rivalen* production in Berlin which opened just eight months after Weill and Brecht's success with *The Threepenny Opera*. *Knickerbocker Holiday* opened on Broadway in 1938 and ran for 168 performances. The production was Weill's first commercial success in America.[55] A closer look at this centennial production will bring the staging of Anderson's work in foreign translation full circle and remind us that Anderson's poetry, language, and social and political commentary are still alive on the world stage.

The Münster production of *Knickerbocker Holiday* was directed by Stephan Mettin in a revival of a musical which is rarely done in America, let alone West Germany. After the considerable success of the Ute and Volker Canaris translation in the 1976 Hamburg production, which was staged as a tribute to America's bicentennial, a revival was well overdue. Certainly, the music is still fresh, with hints of vaudeville tradition giving a nice variety to the score. There is literally something for everyone from the sentimental ballad to the military march, even a bit of the blues. Most critics agreed that Kurt Weill's score raises the level of music a step beyond the usual "ditty" that one finds in many commercial Broadway musicals, especially from that period. The small orchestra played well under the baton of Thomas Modos. Roland Holz as Stuyvesant provided a brash, incorrigible character that dominated the stage and projected a rough humor and a bit of tenderness when he sang "September Song." His stage presence created a strong comic contrast to the bumbling Dutch councilmen who puff away on their long pipes as if they were filled with pot, which, in fact, may explain their roly-poly wit. Münster is situated only a few kilometers from the Dutch border, so the play on the Dutch word puns and accent in German worked exceptionally well for this production. The local Dutch maidens stripped from their long black skirts to white chorus girl ruffles, creating a sort of theatrical conceit in breaking out of the period. This all added to the lively chorus girl nature of the dancing but did not quite complete the potential for real spectacle. The choreography was not that precise and at times seemed a bit muddled. If they were seeking "pizzazz," they lacked vitality.

Olaf Kreutzenbeck as Brom and Ute Heidorn as Tina made a fine loving pair and seemed to touch the heart of the audience with their ballads that are almost like operetta in style, something the Germans do better than most Americans. Kreutzenbeck gave a good sense of a rebel and feeling for the independent American. The lyrics of "How Can You Tell an American?" ("Wie ist der Mann aus America?") revealed this clearly and expressed the undertone of Anderson's satire.

Susanne Klopfstock's design consisted of several unit set pieces on rollers which could be moved into various shapes representing either the jail house or gallows depending on their arrangement. Hanging over the stage were pieces of cloth with primitive tulips painted on them as if they had emerged from a child's fantasy of Holland. Cutouts in the shape of clouds and bordered with blinking lights placed in the center of painted tulips hung over the set. Similarly, cutouts of tulips along the entire front of the proscenium floor provided "blinking tulip bulbs" during transitions and several of the dance sequences.

The German translation by Ute and Volker Canaris worked well and did not distract from the effectiveness of the book and lyrics. In fact, it may be an improvement on the original. Some Americanisms were lost, of course, but conversely, much was gained in the German. This is particularly true of Anderson's political satire which seems to have a more potent effect in German since German audiences are more tuned in to political satire than American audiences. Some critics of the 1976 Hamburg production saw similarities in the "despot" Stuyvesant with Hitler. Curiously, this was perhaps much closer to the concept of the 1938 Anderson and Weill production. But for German audiences the satire of this musical was not biting enough, although Anderson's line "keep government small and funny" was a resounding success.[56]

Although Anderson's works have not maintained foreign popularity equal to those of O'Neill, Wilder, Williams or Albee, nor achieved "classic" status in the eyes of contemporary European critics, the poetic expression of his language, the thematic poignancy of his drama and the international pulse of his worldly characters have engendered an appreciation of his work and challenged leading poets, translators and adaptors in their respective countries to create the essence of that poetry and imagery in the expression of their own language. Likewise, the theatrical imagery and dramatic elements of the plays attracted leading voices of theatres throughout Europe.

Fig. 1 *Knickerbocker Holiday*
Olaf Kreutzenbeck as Brom Broek
Ute Heindorn as Tina Tienhoven

Photo courtesy *Städtische Bühnen Münster*

Fig. 2 *Knickerbocker Holiday*
  Waldemar Stutzmann as Tienhoven
  Roland Holz as Pieter Stuyvesant

Photo courtesy *Städtische Bühnen Münster*

Fig. 3 *Knickerbocker Holiday*
The Ensemble

Photo courtesy *Städtische Bühnen Münster*

Notes

The manuscripts, translations, clipping files, newspapers, promptbooks, reviews, radio scripts and other documents included in the following endnotes are to be found in the Drottningholm Theatre Museum Library (Stockholm), the Royal Dramatic Theatre Archives in Stockholm, the Finnish Centre of the International Theatre Institute in Helsinki, the Deutsches Theatermuseum (Munich), the Bayerische Staatsbibliothek, the Library of the Institut für Theaterwissenschaft at the University of Munich, the Theatermuseum at the University of Cologne, the Institut für Zeitungsforschung in Dortmund, the Städtische Bühnen Münster Archives, the University of Mannheim Library, Library of Congress, Johns Hopkins University Archives, University of Minnesota Library, Bibliothèque National (Paris), and the University of North Dakota Library. The number of foreign productions and the amount of material uncovered in researching this study has far exceeded the scope of this essay. Consequently, a comprehensive bibliography is presently being prepared and will be published in the *North Dakota Quarterly*.

1. *Arbeitsjournal* (Frankfurt: Suhrkamp Verlag, 1973) 153. A newspaper photo of Anderson and Kurt Weill with a pasted on headline clipping saying "Maxwell Anderson Looks for Planes over High Tor" is entered in April 1942: 413.

2. For an overview of German theatre activity during this period see John Willet, *The Theatre of the Weimar Republic* (New York: Holmes & Meier, 1988).

3. Barbara Glaubert, ed., *Carl Zuckmayer: Das Bühnenwerk im Spiegel der Kritik* (Frankfurt: S. Fischer, 1977) 131.

4. Glaubert 131-132. The adaptation does not appear in Zuckmayer's *Gesammelte Werke* 4 vols. (Frankfurt: S. Fischer, 1960) nor *Werkausgaben in zehn Bänden 1920-1975* 10 vols. (Frankfurt: Fischer Taschenbuch Verlag, 1976). It was published as a script edition: *"Rivalen"* (What Price Glory). Ein Stück in

drei Akten (nach dem amerikanischen Schauspiel von Maxwell Anderson und Laurence Stallings)." Berlin: Arcadia-Verlag, 1929. For a comparative analysis see Pauline Steiner and Horst Frenz, "Anderson and Stalling's *What Price Glory* and Carl Zuckmayer's *Rivalen*," *German Quarterly* 20.4 (Nov. 1947): 239-251.

5. "Piscator inszeniert 'Rivalen,'" *Die Rote Fahne* 22 March 1929.

6. Monty Jacobs, "'Rivalen': Theater in der Königgrätzer Strasse," *Vossische Zeitung* 22 March 1929.

7. Max Hochdorf, "Das Kriegsschauspiel 'Rivalen,'" *Der Abend* (late ed. of *Vorwärts*) 21 March 1929.

8. Heinrich Bachmann, "Theater in der Königgrätzer Strasse," *Germania* 21 March 1929, late ed.: 2.

9. Ernst Heilborn, "Erwin Piscator inszeniert...," Frankfurter Zeitung und Handelsblatt 25 March 1929, late ed.

10. Erwin Piscator, *The Political Theater*, Hugh Rorrison, trans, (New York: Avon Books, 1978) 323-324. German original *Das Politische Theater* (Hamburg: Rowohlt Verlag, 1963) 227.

11. See Friedrich Düsel, "Dramatische Rundschau," *Westermanns Monatshefte* 146 (May 1929): 310.

12. C. Hooper Trask, "Broadway Plays Abroad," *New York Times* 28 April 1929, 9: 1-2.

13. Alfred Kerr, "Zuckmayer: 'Rivalen,'" *Berliner Tageblatt* 21 March 1929, late ed.: 2-3.

14. See Steiner and Frenz. See also reviews Paul Fechter, "Der dramatisierte Rivalen Film," *Deutsche Allgemeine Zeitung* (Berlin) 22 March 1929: 1, *Das Theater* 10 (1929): 147, Herbert Jhering, "Theater in der Königgrätzer Strasse," *Berliner Börsen-Courier* 21 March 1929, and Hans Knudsen, "Zuckmayer...Rivalen," *Die schöne Literatur* (Leipzig) 30.5 (May 1929): 235.

15. Trask.

16. *Frankfurter Zeitung* 28 May 1929: 1. Zuckmayer mentions the brawl in his *Als wär's ein Stück von mir* (Vienna: S. Fischer Verlag, 1966) 439. A travel section featuring Berlin recommends *Rivalen* as one of its top choices of plays to see, *Frankfurter Zeitung* 7 July 1929.

17. Arthur Eloesser, "Zaungäste," *Vossische Zeitung* 3 May 1929.

18. Friedrich Düsel, "Dramatische Rundschau," *Westermanns Monatshefte* 146 (June 1929): 412. See also Bruno E. Werner, "Zaungäste," *Deutsche Allgemeine Zeitung* 4 May 1929: 2.

19. See Piscator 329-330. Also *Die Rote Fahne* 23 April 1929 and 24 August 1929.

20. Ernst Lothar, "Feuilleton: Kriegsstückkonjunktur," *Neue Freie Presse* 29 June 1929.

21. "Scen och Film," *Dagens Nyheter* 19 July 1929.

22. "Dramatens premiar: Max. Anderson's 'Ärans fält,'" *Dagens Nyheter* 6 October 1929. See also Carl G. Laurin, *Ros och Ris: Från Stockholms Teatrar 1929-1933*, 5 (Stockholm: P.A. Norstedt, 1933) 93-95; *En bok om Per Lindberg* (Wahlström & Widstrand, 1944) 128-129; "Dramatens krigspjäs," *Stockholms Dagblad* 6 Oct. 1929; "Ärans fält," *Svenska Dagbladet* 6 Oct. 1929; "Krigspremiär på Dramaten," *Stockholms-Tidningen* 6 Oct. 1929; "Ärans fält Dramatens Krigspjäs," *Social-Demokraten* 6 Oct. 1929; "Amerikansk soldatesk pa Dramaten'" *Aftanbladet* 6 Oct. 1929; "Ärans fält," *Arbetaren* 7 Oct. 1929; "Dramatisk stockholmsrevy," *Göteborgs-Posten* 9 Oct. 1929.

23. "'Så'na barn' på Blancheteatern," *Dagen Nyheter* 1 Feb. 1929: 10. See also Laurin 75-76 and Gustaf Collijn, "Maxwell Anderson," *Boniers Litterara Magasin* 9 (Nov. 1940) 689-693; "Så'na barn," *Stockholms Dagblad* 1 Feb. 1929; "Så'na barn," *Svenska Dagbladet* 1 Feb. 1929; "Blancheteatern," *Stockholms-Tidningen* 1 Feb. 1929; *Göteborgs Dagblad* 18 Oct. 1929; Göteborgs Handelstidning 18 Oct. 1929; *Göteborgs-Posten* 18 Oct. 1929.

24. Stanislaw Marczak-Oborski, *Teatr w Polsce 1918-1939* (Warsaw: Państwowy Instytut Wydawniczy, 1984) 145.

25. Stanislaw Marczak-Oborski, *Teatr polski w latach 1918- 1965* (Warsaw: Państwowe Wydawnictwo Naukowe, 1985) 90-91.

26. Czeslaw Milosz, *The History of Polish Literature* (Berkeley: U of California P, 1983) 2nd ed.: 354, 414.

27. Henry A. Diez, "Vienna Stages Anderson Play as U.S. Classic," *New York Herald Tribune* 9 Nov. 1935.

28. For the complete cast list see *Burgtheater 1776-1976: Aufführungen und Besetzungen von zweihundert Jahren* 1 (Vienna: Salzer-Uebereuter, 1978) 575. It is somewhat ironic that the theme of the "U.S. Classic" is distinctly a British subject.

29. "Nationaltheatret. Maxwell Anderson: 'Mot vår,'" *Morgenbladet*, Oslo, 4 Oct. 1934: 4.

30. Anton Rønneberg, *Nationaltheatret Gjennom Femti År* 2 (Oslo: Gyldendal Norske Forlag, 1949) 358-359.

31. Finn Halvorsen, "Det Norske Teatret: Maxwell Anderson: 'High Tor,'" *Morgenbladet* 19 Feb. 1940: 4. See also "Maxwell Anderson—premiere på Det Norske Teatret iaften," *Morgenbladet* 15 Oct. 1940: 3.

32. Anton Rønneberg, *Teater: Hjemme og Ute* (Oslo: H. Aschehoug, 1945) 209, 231-234.

33. "Mayerlingdramats' premiär," *Dagens Nyheter* 8 Oct. 1938: 1. See also Gunmar Lundin and Jan Olsson, *Rigissörens Roller samtal med Alf Sjöberg* (Lund: Bo Cavefors Bokförlag, 1976); "Mayerlingdramat på svensk scen," *Aftonbladet* 8 Oct. 1938; "Frän Dramatens premiär," *Arbetaren* 8 Oct. 1938; "Mayerlingdramat pä Dramaten," *Social-Demokraten* 8 Oct. 1938; "Mayerling på Dramaten," *Stockholms-Tidningen* 8 Oct. 1938; "Mayerlingdramat på Dramaten," *Svenska Dagbladet* 8 Oct. 1938; "Mayerlingdramat," *Göteborgs Handelstidning* 10 Oct. 1938; *Göteborgs Posten* 11 Oct. 1938.

34. Collijn 389; "Star ispelkvall på Dramaten," *Dagens Nyheter* 16 Oct. 1943; "Vi har vår frihet," *Social- Demokraten* 16 Oct. 1943; "Vi har vår frihet," *Svenska Dagbladet* Oct. 1943; "Vi har vår frihet, *Stockholms-Tidningen* 16 Oct. 1943; *Göteborgs Tidningen* 16 Oct. 1943; "En Shakespeare på Amerikanska," *Upsala Nya Tidning* 16 Oct. 1943; "Maxwell Anderson's nya Krigspjäs på Dramaten," *Göteborgs Handelstidning* 19 Oct. 1943; *Göteborgs Dagblad* 20 Oct. 1943; "Maxwell Anderson," *Aftonbladet* 16 Oct. 1943.

35. "Morgondagens män på Dramaten," *Dagens Nyheter* 5 Oct. 1940; Photos of set, *Social-Demokraten* 2 Oct. 1940; "Morgondagens män på Dramaten," *Aftonbladet* 5 Oct. 1940; "Dramaten: M.m.," *Social-Demokraten* 5 Oct. 1940; "Märkligt skådespel på Dramaten," *Svenska Dagbladet* 5 Oct. 1940; "Morgondagens män," *Stockholms-Tidningen* 5 Oct. 1940; "MA Key Largo,"

Göteborgs Dagblad 9 Oct. 1940; "Europeisk urpremiär på Dramaten," *Morgontidning* 8 Oct. 1940.

36. "Natt över New York," *Göteborgs Dagblad* 17 March 1937; "Natt över New York," *Göteborgs Handelstidning* 17 March 1937; "Natt över New York," *Göteborgs Posten* 17 March 1937; "Morgondagens män," *Göteborgs Dagblad* 26 Feb. 1941; "Morgondagens män," *Morgontidningen* (Gothenburg) 26 Feb. 1937.

37. See Ingrid Qvarnstrom, *Svensk Teater i Finland* 2 (Stockholm: Wahlström & Widstrand, 1947). See also Lundin.

38. *Enciclopedia dello Spettacolo* 1 (Rome: Casa Editrice Le Maschere, 1954) 530-534.

39. Giorgio Strehler, *Für ein menschlicheres Theater* (Frankfurt: Suhrkamp, 1975) 28. Original ed. *Per un teatro umano. Pensiere scritti parlati e attuati* (Milan: Giangiacomb Feltrinelli, 1974).

40. Paul Surer, *Le Théâtre Français Contemporain* (Paris: Société d'Edition d'Enseignement Supérieur, 1964) 141-148.

41. Ilse Urbach, "Die Heilige Johanna aus USA," *Die Welt* 12 March 1953. See photo *Die Welt* 11 March 1953. Also O.B. Lomow, "Johanna wird re-europäisiert," *Frankfurter Allgemeine Zeitung* 12 March 1953.

42. Fritz Heerwagen, "'Anna, Königin für tausend Tage': Deutsche Erstaufführung in Düsseldorf," *Frankfurter Allgemeine Zeitung* 8 Nov. 1950: 6. See Rolf Trauwborst, "Die Düsseldorfer Zeit 1947-1955," in *Gründgens* (Hannover: Erhard Friedrich Verlag, 1963) 60.

43. Critics found the use of verse by the characters unconvincing. Oskar Maurus Fontana, *Die Presse* 25 March 1956: 8. Also Hans Weigel, *Bild-Telegraf* 24 March 1956.

44. "'Key Largo' har premiere på Nationaltheatret," *Morgenbladet* 22 Oct. 1946: 5. Photo in *Morgenbladet* 23 Oct. 1946: 3. Review, "Aktuell Maxwell Anderson på Nationaltheatret," *Morgenbladet* 25 Oct. 1946: 3-4. Also see Rønneberg, *Nationaltheatret* 442.

45. Carl Fredrik Engelstad, "Mayerlingdramaet på Nationaltheatret," *Morgenbladet* 8 August 1953. Also Anton Rønneberg, *National-theatret 1949-1974* (Oslo: Gyldendal Norske Forlag, 1974) 75.

46. Production photo, "*The Wingless Victory*," *Theatre Arts Monthly* 24 (May 1945): 309. Photo of Wållgren as Joan in Gustaf Hillestrom, *Theatre and Ballet in Sweden*, Anne Bibby, trans. (Stockholm: The Swedish Institute, 1953). *Anne* reviews: "Kungapar på Dramaten," *Stockholms-Tidningen* 8 Dec. 1949; *Svenska Dagbladet* 8 Dec. 1949; "Fyra timmar följetong," *Arbetaren* 8 Dec. 1949; "MA's 'En d.a.t.' på Dramt.," *Dagsposten* 8 Dec. 1949; "Moderniserad renässans på Dramaten," *Aftonbladet* 8 Dec. 1949; "MA på Dramaten," *Göteborgs Tidningen* 8 Dec. 1949; "MA på Dramt.," *Göteborgs Morgonpost* 18 Dec. 1949; "Teater, musik och film," *Svenska Dagbladet* 9 Dec. 1949; "Thalia i orubbat bo," *Medborgaren* (Stockholm) 6 Jan. 1950.

47. See *Göteborgs Dagblad* 26 Feb. 1941 and 8 Feb. 1948; *Göteborgs Tidningen* 26 Feb. 1941 and 8 Feb. 1948.

48. "'Joan of Lorraine' In Athens Premiere," *New York Herald Tribune* 14 Nov. 1947: 19.

49. *Enciclopedia dello Spettacolo* 530-534.

50. "Kulturelle Notizen," *Frankfurter Allgemeine Zeitung* 1 Nov. 1950: 6.

51. The manuscripts for these radio adaptations are in the Drottningholms Teatermuseum in Stockholm. Several of the manuscripts are without dates.

52. Ole Øisang, *Trøndelag Teater: Gjennom 25 år* (Trondheim: F. Bruns Bokhandels, 1962) 169-170.

53. Gerd Klepzig, "'*Knickerbocker Holiday*' bekam nur durch geglückte Inszenierung Halt," *Die Welt* 27 Sept. 1976. Also Klaus Wagner, "Plädoyer für den amerikanischen 'Weill,'" *Frankfurter Allgemeine Zeitung* 29 Sept. 1976: 23.

54. For an analysis of the following Anderson plays in German see Jerôme von Gebsattel, "*Elizabeth the Queen*," *Kindlers Literatur Lexikon [KLL]* 2 (Zürich: Kindler Verlag, 1965) 2000, Gebsattel, "*Joan of Lorraine*," *KLL* 4: 7, Gebsattel, "*Key Largo*," *KLL* 4: 460, and Michael Köhler, "*Winterset*," 7: 1172. See also Margaret Dietrich, *Das Moderne Drama* (Stuttgart: Alfred Kröner, 1963) 21, 500, 503f, 642, 648, 685, 686.

55. See Ronald Sanders, *The Days Grow Short: The Life and Music of Kurt Weill* (New York: Holt, 1980) 269-282 for a full account of the Broadway production. Note that Sanders has mistaken Reinhardt for Piscator in reference to *What Price Glory*, 270. See also Jürgen Schebera, *Kurt Weill: Leben und Werk* (Leipzig: Athenäum Verlag, 1984) 183-242. Also Alfred S. Shivers *The*

Life of Maxwell Anderson (New York: Stein, 1983) and Laurence G. Avery, *Dramatist in America: Letters of Maxwell Anderson, 1912-1958* (Chapel Hill: U of NC Press, 1977). A brief synopsis and song list in both English and German is in Stephan Pflicht, *Musical-Führer* (Mainz: B. Schott's Söhne, 1980) 165-167. A handwritten copy of the original *Knickerbocker Holiday* manuscript is in the Maxwell Anderson Collection at the University of North Dakota Chester Fritz Library and also at the University of Texas.

56. See Ron Engle, "West Germans Celebrate North Dakota's Most Famous Playwright," Grand Forks Herald 1 July 1988. Also reviews in *Die Glocke* 6 Feb. 1988, *Westfälische Nachrichten* 6 Feb. 1988, and *Hannoversche Allgemeine* 6 Feb. 1988.

Appendix

Maxwell Anderson productions in foreign translation on the European stage 1929-1988

PLAY	DATE	THEATRE	COUNTRY/CITY	REMARKS
		AUSTRIA		
What Price Glory [*Rivalen*]	8 June 1929	Städtische Bühnen, Schauspielhaus	Graz	Carl Zuckmayer, trans.
What Price Glory [*Rivalen*]	28 June 1929	Deutsches Volkstheater	Vienna	Carl Zuckmayer, trans., Heinz Hilpert, dir., Alfred Kunz, design. Cast: Roma Bahn, Hans Hinrich, Hans Olden, Karl Forest & Otto Schmöle.
Elizabeth the Queen [*Elisabeth und Essex*]	8 Nov. 1935 (13 perfs.)	Burgtheater	Vienna	Friedrich Schreyvogel, trans. Cast: Maria Eis & Heinz Woester.
Joan of Lorraine [*Johanna von Lothringen*]	1954/55 Season (6 perfs.)	Theater in der Josefstadt	Vienna	Walter Firner, trans.
Winterset [*Winterwende*]	23 March 1956 (9 perfs.)	Volkstheater	Vienna	Hans Sahl, trans., Leon Epp, dir., Gustav Mankers, design. Cast: Günther Haenels, Kurt Sowinetz, Maria Urban, Ernst Meister & Benno Smytt.
Anne of the Thousand Days [*Anna, Königin für tausend Tage*]	19 Dec. 1963	Volkstheater	Vienna	Friedrich Schreyvogel, trans.
		CZECHOSLOVAKIA		
What Price Glory [*Rivalen*]	21 Sept. 1929	Vereinigte Deutsche Theater, Schauspielhaus	Brünn [Now Brno]	Carl Zuckmayer, trans., German language production.
What Price Glory [*Rivalen*]	26 Oct. 1929	Neues deutsches Theater	Prague	Carl Zuckmayer, trans., Max Liebl, dir. Cast: Waldemar Leitgeb, Josef Renner & Irene Lamond.

Maxwell Anderson

PLAY	DATE	THEATRE	COUNTRY/CITY	REMARKS
Czechoslovakia (continued)				
What Price Glory [*Rivalen*]	7 Nov. 1929	Stadttheater	Brüx [Now Most]	Carl Zuckmayer, trans., Franz Schramm, Intendant [Manager/Director].
FINLAND				
Saturday's Children [*Sä'na barn*]	11 April 1929 (16 perfs.)	Svenska Teatern	Helsinki	(S = Swedish language perf./F = Finnish language perf.] (S) Gustaf Collijn, trans.
What Price Glory [*Länsirintamalla*]	5 March 1930	Tampereen Työväen Teatteri	Tampere	(F)
What Price Glory [*Kunnian kentällä*]	1934/35	Turun *Työväen Teatteri*	Turku	(F)
The Masque of Kings [*Furstemasker*]	3 Jan. 1939 (14 perfs.)	Svenska Teatern	Helsinki	(S) Karl Ragnar Gierow, trans. Cast: Erik Lindströms.
Winterset [*New Yorkin nukkuessa*]	1945/46 (19 perfs.)	Helsingin Kansanteatteri	Helsinki	(F)
Winterset [*New Yorkin nukkuessa*]	1945/46 (9 perfs.)	Tampereen Teatteri	Tampere	(F)
Winterset [*New Yorkin nukkuessa*]	1947/48 (5 perfs.)	Valkeakosken Työväen Näyttämö	Valkeakoski	(F)
Saturday's Children [*Lauantailapsia*]	1947/48 (7 perfs.)	Helsingin Työväen Teatteri	Helsinki	(F)
Joan of Lorraine [*Lothringenin Johanna*]	1947/48 (18 perfs.) 1948/49 (11 perfs.)	Suomen Kansallisteatteri (Finnish Nat. Theatre)	Helsinki	(F)
Joan of Lorraine [*Johanna från Lothringen*]	19 May 1948 (14 perfs.)	Svenska Teatern	Helsinki	(S) Herbert Grevenius, trans.

137

R. Engle

PLAY	DATE	THEATRE	COUNTRY/CITY	REMARKS
Finland (continued)				
Joan of Lorraine [*Lothringenin Johanna*]	1948/49 (9 perfs.)	Tampereen Teatteri	Tampere	(F)
Joan of Lorraine [*Lothringenin Johanna*]	1948/49 (11 perfs.)	Porin Teatteri	Pori	(F)
Joan of Lorraine [*Lothringenin Johanna*]	1948/49 (23 perfs.)	Turun Kaupungin-teatteri	Turku	(F)
Joan of Lorraine [*Lothringenin Johanna*]	1948/49 (9 perfs.)	Hämeenlinnan Työväen Teatteri	Hämeenlinna	(F)
Joan of Lorraine [*Lothringenin Johanna*]	1949/50 (9 perfs.)	Jyväskylän Työväen Teatteri	Jyväskylä	(F)
Knickerbocker Holiday [*Riemunpäivä*]	1949/50 (6 perfs.)	Helsingin Kansan-teatteri-Työväen-teatteri	Helsinki	(F)
Winterset [*New York nukkuessa*]	1950/51 (4 perfs.)	Kymin Työväen Yhteisteatteri		(F)
Anne of the Thousand Days [*Päivä tuhannesta*]	1951/52 (25 perfs.)	Suomen Kansallis-teatteri (Finnish Nat. Theatre)	Helsinki	(F)
Anne of the Thousand Days [*Päivä tuhannesta*]	1951/52 (12 perfs.)	Tampereen Teatteri	Tampere	(F)
Key Largo [*Morgondagens män*]	26 Feb. 1957 (17 perfs.)	Svenska Teatern	Helsinki	(S) Artur Lundkvist, trans.
FRANCE				
Winterset	26 Jan. 1946	Théâtre des Carrefours	Paris	Marcel Achard, trans., Jean Serge, dir., Roger Dornès, design, Jean Wiener, music. Cast: Daniel Gélin, Yves Vincent & Marie Carlot.

138

Maxwell Anderson

PLAY	DATE	THEATRE	COUNTRY/CITY	REMARKS
		GERMANY		
What Price Glory [*Rivalen*]	20 March 1929	Theater in der Königgrätzer Strasse	Berlin	Carl Zuckmayer, trans., Erwin Piscator, dir., Caspar Neher, design. Cast: Fritz Kortner, Hans Albers & Maria Bard.
What Price Glory [*Rivalen*]	13 April 1929 27 April 1929	Lobe-Theater Thalia theater [Moved from/to]	Breslau [Now Wroclaw Poland]	Carl Zuckmayer, trans., Paul Barnay, Intendant [Artistic Director].
Outside Looking In [*Zaungäste*]	30 April 1929	Schiller Theater	Berlin	Rita Matthias & L. Keneth, trans.., Jürgen Fehling, dir., Rochus Gliese, design. Cast: Ruth Albu, Paul Bildt, Aribert Wäscher, Julius Falkenstein & Veit Harlan.
What Price Glory [*Rivalen*]	6 May 1929	Schauspielhaus	Dresden	Carl Zuckmayer, trans., H.W. Litten, dir.
What Price Glory [*Rivalen*]	15 June 1929	Schauspielhaus	Düsseldorf	Carl Zuckmayer, trans., Peter Scharoff, dir., Eduard Sturm, design. Cast: Otto Ernst Lundt & Harry Flatow.
What Price Glory [*Rivalen*]	20 June 1929	Landestheater	Oldenburg	Carl Zuckmayer, trans.
What Price Glory [*Rivalen*]	9 August 1929	Intimes Theater	Nürnberg	Carl Zuckmayer, trans.., Hanns Schindler, dir. Cast: Willi Bankel, Hanns Schindler & Lydia Barth.
What Price Glory [*Rivalen*]	13 Sept. 1929	Schauspielhaus	Bremen	Carl Zuckmayer, trans.
What Price Glory [*Rivalen*]	19 Sept. 1929	Schauspielhaus	Chemnitz	Carl Zuckmayer, trans., H.W. Litten, dir.
What Price Glory [*Rivalen*]	28 Sept. 1929	Städtisches Theater, Altes Haus	Leipzig	Carl Zuckmayer, trans., Erich Schönlank, dir. Cast: Robert Meyn, Gerhard Ritter & Ruth Hellberg.

R. Engle

PLAY	DATE	THEATRE	COUNTRY/CITY	REMARKS
		Germany (continued)		
What Price Glory [*Rivalen*]	30 Sept. 1929	Neues Schauspielhaus der Jadestädte	Wilhelmshaven Rustringen	Carl Zuckmayer, trans., Robert Hellwig, Int.
What Price Glory [*Rivalen*]	8 Oct. 1929	Deutsches Theater	Hannover	Carl Zuckmayer, trans., Hanns Schindler, guest dir. (Nürnberg) Cast: Hanns Schindler, Lydia Barth & Hans v. Zedlitz (guest/Berlin).
What Price Glory [*Rivalen*]	19 Oct. 1929	Neues Theater	Frankfurt a.M.	Carl Zuckmayer, trans., Renato Mordo, dir. Cast: Rudolf Basil, Theo Lingen & Lydia Busch.
What Price Glory [*Rivalen*]	23 Oct. 1929	Kammerspiele	Hamburg	Carl Zuckmayer, trans., Erich Ziegel, dir. Cast: Ernst Fritz Fürbringer, Albrecht Schoenhals, Hans Stiebner, Walter Gussmann & Anneliese Born.
What Price Glory [*Rivalen*]	2 Nov. 1929	Schauspielhaus	Dortmund	Carl Zuckmayer, trans., Richard Gsell, dir., Giskes, design. Cast: Lütjohann, Semmt, Kulisch, Feuerherd, Dewald & Knaack.
What Price Glory [*Rivalen*]	26 Nov. 1929	Stadttheater	Hagen	Carl Zuckmayer, trans.
What Price Glory [*Rivalen*]	12 March 1930	Stadttheater	Augsburg	Carl Zuckmayer, trans., Hans Abrell, dir. Cast: Adolf Rehbach, Gert Benofsky & Grete Safar.
Outside Looking In [*Zaungäste*]	13 March 1930	Kammerspiele	Hamburg	Rita Matthias & L. Keneth, trans., Hans Lotz, dir., Johannes Schröder, design. Cast: Ernst Fritz, Fürbringer, Eugen Klimm, Hans Stiebner & Doris Kiesow.

Maxwell Anderson

PLAY	DATE	THEATRE	COUNTRY/CITY	REMARKS
		Germany (continued)		
What Price Glory [*Rivalen*]	24 March 1930	Kammerspiele	Munich	Carl Zuckmayer, trans. Cast: Ewald Balser, Dohm & Ehmi Bessel.
What Price Glory [*Rivalen*]	24 April 1930	Hessisches Landestheater, Grosses Haus	Darmstadt	Carl Zuckmayer, trans., Arthur Maria Rebenalt, dir., Walter Auerbach, design. Cast: Werner Hinz, Siegfried Nürnberger, Bessie Hoffart & Franz Plaudler.
Gods of the Lightning [*Und wir haben nichts dagegen getan*]	20 Sept. 1930	Kammerspiele	Hamburg	Konrad Maril, trans., Mirjam Horwitz, dir. Cast: Ernst Fritz Fürbringer, Albrecht Schoenhals, Maria Loja & Karl Heinz Schroth.
What Price Glory [*Rivalen*]	17 Nov. 1930	Stadttheater	Brieg [Now Brzeg in Poland]	Carl Zuckmayer, trans., Hugo Friedrich, Int.
What Price Glory [*Rivalen*]	2 March 1934	Theater im Admiralspalast	Berlin	Carl Zuckmayer, trans., Jakob Geis, dir., Caspar Neher, design, Hanns Steinkopf, music. Cast: Hans Albers, Leopold Biberti [as Flagg, later replaced by Hans Schulze], Jessy Vihrog, Ernst Legal, Egon Brosig, Paul Westermeier & Karl Reiner.
Saturday's Children [*Leute wie Du und ich*]	13 Sept. 1947	Junge Bühne	Hamburg	Maria Teichs, trans., Paul Smolny, dir., Hannelore Schipmann, design. Cast: Lidy Schwieder, Hans Richter, Walter Kohls, Evelyn Peters & Walter Falk.
Saturday's Children [*Leute wie Du und ich*]	24 Jan. 1947	Theater der Jugend	Stuttgart	Maria Teichs, trans. Cast: Eva Thomson, Kurt Müller-Graf & Gerda Maria Jürgens.

141

R. Engle

PLAY	DATE	COUNTRY/CITY	THEATRE	REMARKS
Germany (continued)				
Saturday's Children [*Leute wie Du und ich*]	5 March 1947	Memmingen	Stadttheater	Maria Teichs, trans., Wilhelm Allgayer, dir., Franz Dransfeld, design. Cast: Gertrud Jarand, Dietlinde Fritsch, Albert Loesnau, & Heinz Heissler.
Mary of Scotland [*Mary von Schottland*]	5 March 1947	Stuttgart	Württembergisches Staatstheater, Kammertheater	Katrin Janecke & Günter Blöcker, trans., Hermine Körner, dir., Friedhelm Strenger, design, Asta Ruth, cost., Hellmut Löffler, music. Cast: Gisela Uhlen, Maria Wiecke & Friedrich Schönfelder.
Saturday's Children [*Leute wie Du und ich*]	[15] April 1947	Munich	Neues Theater	Maria Teichs, trans., Ulrich Beiger, dir., Marleen Pacha, design. Cast: Anja Wernicke & August Riehl.
Mary of Scotland [*Maria von Schottland*]	25 March 1948	Memmingen	Stadttheater	Katrin Janecke & Günter Blöcker, trans., Erich Schmidt, dir., Heinrich Siebald, design, Herrmann Hausmann, cost. Cast: Dietlinde Fritsch, Eleonore Götz, Gustav Rothe, Kurt Marquardt, Erich Schmidt & Heinz Heissler.
Knickerbocker Holiday [*Knickerbockers*]	25 Nov. 1948	Essen	Städtische Bühnen	Katharina Heinsius & Johannes Stephan, trans., Klaus Heydenreich, dir. Cast: Ingeborg Engelmann, Horst Braun & Ernst Walter Mitulski.
Knickerbocker Holiday [*Knickerbockers*]	[1948]	Berlin, West	Hebbel-Theater	Katharina Heinsius & Johannes Stephan, trans.

Maxwell Anderson

PLAY	DATE	THEATRE	COUNTRY/CITY	REMARKS
		Germany (continued)		
Anne of the Thousand Days [*Anna, Königin für tausend Tage*]	2 Nov. 1950	Stadttheater Neues Theater	Düsseldorf	Friedrich Schreyvogel, trans., Ulrich Erfurth, dir., Hertha Boehm, design & cost. Cast: Marianne Hoppe & Gerhard Geisler
Joan of Lorraine [*Johanna aus Lothringen*]	10 March 1953	Kammerspiele	Hamburg	Walter Firner, trans. and dir., Heinz Hoffmann, design. Cast: Hilde Krahl, Wolfgang Liebeneiner, & Richard Muench.
Joan of Lorraine [*Johanna aus Lothringen*]	12 Feb. 1954	Städtische Bühnen	Gelsenkirchen	Walter Firner, trans., Jost Dahmen, dir. Cast: Irene Dodel & Reimser Krönung.
What Price Glory [*Rivalen*]	5 Jan. 1955	Städtische Bühnen	Cologne	Carl Zuckmayer, trans., Herbert Maisch, dir., W. Gondolf, design. Cast: Kaspar Brüninghaus, Gerhard Becker, Edith Teichmann & Heinz Schacht.
Joan of Lorraine [*Johanna aus Lothringen*]	1 Feb. 1955	Landestheater	Coburg	Walter Firner, trans., Rudolf Biedermann, dir., Fritz Mahnke, design, Nina Kemper, cost. Cast: Sigrid Noell, Rudolf Biedermann, Günter Mack, Joachim Böse, Raymond Joob, Alexander Deissner, & Peter Horn.
Winterset [*Wintertag*]	22 Dec. 1955	Städtische Bühnen	Essen	Hans Sahl, trans., Gerhard Reuter, dir., Friedhelm Strenger, design. Cast: Beatrice Föhr-Waldeck, Günther Tabor, Wolfgang Schirlitz & Hans-Karl Friedrich.

143

R. Engle

PLAY	DATE	COUNTRY/CITY	THEATRE	REMARKS
Germany (continued)				
Barefoot in Athens [*Barfuss in Athen*]	10 Jan. 1957	Hamburg	Thalia Theater	Hans Sahl, trans., Imo Moszkowicz, dir., Fritz Brauer, design. Cast: Charlotte Kramm & Heinz Klevenow.
Knickerbocker Holiday	25 Sept. 1976 (25 perfs.)	Hamburg	Thalia Theater's TiK-Theater in der Kunsthalle	Ute & Volker Canaris, trans., Helmut Baumann, dir., Jens-Peter Ostendorf, music dir., Kathrin Kegler, design. Cast: Klaus Dittmann, Richard Münch, Axel Radler, Beatrice Richter, Konrad Krauss & Manfred Steffen.
Knickerbocker Holiday	4 February 1988	Münster	Städtische Bühnen Münster	Ute & Volker Canaris, trans., Stephan Mettin, dir., Thomas Modos, music dir., Susanne Klopfstock, design & cost. Cast: Olaf Kreutzenbeck, Ute Heidorn & Roland Holz.
GREECE				
Joan of Lorraine	12 Nov. 1947	Athens		Theodore Kritas, dir. Cast: Vasse Manolidou.
ITALY				
Winterset	1940	Rome	Teatro delle Arti	A. G. Bragaglia, dir.
Star Wagon [*Viaggio alle Stelle*]	1941	Rome	Teatro Eliseo	
Winterset	1946	Milan	Teatro Odeon	Giorgio Strehler, dir. Cast: E. Maltagliati & S. Randone
Joan of Lorraine [*Giovanna di Lorena*]	1949	Rome	P.T. di Roma	O. Costa, dir.

PLAY	DATE	THEATRE	COUNTRY/CITY	REMARKS
Italy (continued)				
Anne of the Thousand Days [*Anna per mille giorni*]	1951	Teatro Valli With Compagnia del Teatro Nazionale	Rome	Guido Salvini, dir., Giulio Coltellacci, design & cost. Cast: V. Gioi & V. Gassman.
LATVIA				
What Price Glory [*Rivalen*]	4 Dec. 1929	Deutsches Schauspielhaus	Riga [Now USSR]	Carl Zuckmayer, trans., Fredrich Mark, Int.
Gods of the Lightning [*Melnais tribunals*] "Black Tribunal"	16 Feb. 1930	Strādnieku Teatris Riga [Worker's Theatre]		Arvīds Grigulis, trans., [Latvian], Olga Bormane, dir., M. Jo, design, Aleksandrs Melli, music. Cast: Luis Smidts, Kārlis Grasbergs, Lucija Baumanis, L. Leimanis, Nikolajs Mūrnieks & Girts Bumblers.
LITHUANIA				
What Price Glory [*Rivalen*]	5 Oct. 1929	Städtisches Schauspielhaus	Memel [Now Klaipedia, USSR]	Heinrich Albers, Int. German language production.
NORWAY				
Winterset [*Mot vår*]	3 Oct. 1939 (8 perfs.)	Nationaltheatret	Oslo	Cast: Arne Bang Hansen & Vibeke Falk.
High Tor	18 Feb. 1940	Det Norske Teatret	Oslo	Samuel Besekow, dir., Arne Walentin, design. Cast: Harald Heide Steen, Tordis Maurstad & Eva Sletsos.
Key Largo	24 Oct. 1946 (8 perfs.)	Nationaltheatret	Oslo	Inger Hagerups, trans., Knut Hergel, dir. Cast: Knut Wigert, Helen Brinchmann, Henrik Børseth Kolbjørn Buøen & Ola Isene.

R. Engle

PLAY	DATE	THEATRE	COUNTRY/CITY	REMARKS
		Norway (continued		
The Masque of Kings [*Mayerlingdramaet*]	7 Aug. 1953 (14 perfs.)	Nationaltheatret	Oslo	Ellen Isefiaer, dir. Cast: Kolbjørn Buøen, Ada Kramm, Børseth Rasmussen & Bab Christensen.
Knickerbocker Holiday	30 May 1960 (60 perfs.)	Trøndelag Teater	Trondheim	Jack Fjeldstad, dir., Jan Berg, music dir., Erna Gulbrandsen, Choreog. Cast: Andreas Bjarke.
		POLAND		
What Price Glory [*Rywale*]	28 Sept. 1929	Teatr Miejski	Lodz	Based on Zuckmayer trans., Leon Schiller, dir., Konstanty Mackiewicz, design. Cast: Jacek Woszczerowicz.
What Price Glory [*Rywale*]	1929/30	Teatr Polski	Warsaw	Arnold Szyfman, dir. Based on Zuckmayer trans.
Winterset [*Sceneria zimowa*]	1967	N/A	Warsaw	N/A
		SWEDEN		
Saturday's Children [*Sä'na barn*]	31 Jan. 1929 (48 perfs.)	Blanche Theatre (Blancheteatern)	Stockholm	Gustaf Collijn, trans., Erik Berglund, dir. Cast: Esther Roeck Hansen & Erik Berglund.
What Price Glory [*Ärans Fält*]	5 Oct. 1929 to 8/11 (21 perfs.)	Royal Dramatic Theatre (Dramaten)	Stockholm	Ture Nerman, trans., Per Lindberg, dir., Sandrow Malmquist, design. Cast: Harriet Bosse, Sven Bergvall, Lars Hanson & Anders Hendrikson.
Saturday's Children [*Sä'na barn*]	17 Oct. 1929 (20 perfs.)	Folkteatern, Lorensberg	Gothenburg	Olof Sandborg, dir.
Winterset [*Natt över New York*]	16 March 1937 (13 perfs.)	Göteborgs Stadsteater	Gothenburg	Knut Ström, dir. & design.

146

Maxwell Anderson

PLAY	DATE	THEATRE	COUNTRY/CITY	REMARKS
Sweden (continued)				
Masque of Kings [*Mayerlingdramat*]	7 Oct. 1938 to 27/11 (32 perfs.)	Royal Dramatic Theatre (Dramaten)	Stockholm	Karl Ragnar Gierow, trans., Alf Sjöberg, dir., Sven Erik Skawonius, design. Cast: Gösta Ekman, Lars Hanson, Tora Teje, Inga Tidblad & Georg Rydeberg.
Winterset [*Grå gryning*]	5 Sept. 1940 to 9/10 (35 perfs.)	New Theatre (Nya teater)	Stockholm	Per-Axel Branner, dir., Erik Söderberg, design.
Key Largo [*Morgondagens män*]	4 Oct. 1940 to 31/10 (27 perfs.)	Royal Dramatic Theatre (Dramaten)	Stockholm	Artur Lundquist, trans., Alf Sjöberg, dir., Sven Erik Skawonius, design. Cast: Lars Hanson & Inga Tidblad.
Key Largo [*Morgondagens män*]	25 Feb. 1941 (17 perfs.)	Göteborgs Stadsteater	Gothenburg	Torsten Hammaren, dir., Knut Ström, design.
The Eve of St. Mark [*Vi har vår frihet*]	15 Oct. 1943 to 26/12 (36 perfs.)	Royal Dramatic Theatre (Dramaten)	Stockholm	Sven Barthel, trans., Olof Molander, dir., Sven Erik Skawonius, design. Cast: Olof Widgren & Anna Lindahl.
The Wingless Victory [*Den obevingade segern*]	28 Nov. 1944 to 17/12 (20 perfs.)	Blanche Theatre (Blancheteatern)	Stockholm	Einar Malm, trans., Sam Besekow, dir., Harald Garmland, design. Cast: Esther Roeck Hansen.
Joan of Lorraine [*Flickan från Lothringen*]	7 Feb. 1948 (37 perfs.)	Göteborgs Stadsteater	Gothenburg	Knut Ström, dir. & design.
Joan of Lorraine [*Johanna från Lothringen*]	3 Sept. 1948 to 20/3/49 (73 perfs.)	Royal Dramatic Theatre (Dramaten)	Stockholm	Herbert Grevenius, trans., Olof Molander, dir., Georg Magnusson, design, Marik Vos, cost. Cast: Gunn Wällgren.
Joan of Lorraine [*Flickan från Lothringen*]	10 Oct. 1948 (4 perfs.)	Göteborgs Stadsteater	Gothenburg	Revival of 7/2/48

R. Engle

PLAY	DATE	THEATRE	COUNTRY/CITY	REMARKS
Sweden (continued)				
Knickerbocker Holiday [*Pä Manhattan*]	1 Jan. 1949 (29 perfs.)	Göteborgs Stadsteater	Gothenburg	Knut Ström, dir. & design.
Anne of the Thousand Days [*En dag av tusen*]	7 Dec. 1949 (43 perfs.)	Royal Dramatic Theatre (Dramaten)	Stockholm	Olof Molander, dir., Georg Magnusson, design, Marik Vos, cost.
Anne of the Thousand Days [*En dag av tusen*]	3 March 1950 (28 perfs.)	Göteborgs Stadsteater	Gothenburg	Helge Wahlgren, dir. Cast: Birgit Afzelius-Wärnlöf.
Winterset [*Storstadsnatt*]	8 Dec. 1955 (12 perfs.)	Folkets Hus Teater	Gothenburg	Erik Söderberg, dir. & design.
The Bad Seed [*Ont blod*[	5 April 1957 (27 perfs.)	Alleteater	Stockholm	Per-Axel Branner, dir., Yngve Gramlin, design.
SWITZERLAND				
What Price Glory [*Rivalen*]	7 Oct. 1929	Stadttheater	Bern	Carl Zuckmayer, trans., Hans Kaufmann, Int.
What Price Glory [*Rivalen*]	24 Oct. 1929	Schauspielhaus	Zurich	Carl Zuckmayer, trans., Herbert Waniek, dir., W. Huller, design. Cast: Schürenberg, Bergmann & Lisi Scherbak.
What Price Glory [*Rivalen*]	4 Sept. 1930	Stadttheater	Basel	Carl Zuckmayer, trans.
Joan of Lorraine [*Johanna aus Lothringen*]	1953	Städtebundtheater	Zurich	Walter Firner, trans. & dir., Ary Oechslin, design. Cast: Ellen Schwanneke.
Winterset [*Winterwende*]	1 March 1956	Schauspielhaus	Zurich	Hans Sahl, trans., Kurt Hirschfeld, dir., Teo Otto, design. Cast: Peter Brogle, Miriam Spoerri, Ernst Ginsbergs, Benna Gerzenbach & Pinkas Braun.

Interview with George Schaefer,

Chair of the Department of Theater, Film, and Television, UCLA.

by Arthur Friedman ,
University of California, Los Angeles

This interview, which is excerpted below, took place on 9 March 1988; Professor Schaefer discusses the University of California, Los Angeles production of *Winterset* that he was then directing. A video of the interview in its entirety is available from the Maxwell Anderson Centennial Committee, Rockland Community College/SUNY.

Friedman: On March 4th, 5th, and 6th...Maxwell Anderson's Winterset was performed on main stage, directed by George Schaefer.... George, I want to welcome you, and ask you, please, how did you settle on Winterset as your inaugural directing chore at UCLA?

Schaefer: Well, that's an easy question to answer, Art. I've been enamored of *Winterset* for more years than I hate to mention. It was originally written and performed in, I guess, about '35-'36, at which time I would have been 15-16 years old, and very impressionable. I did not see the production in New York, nor did I see it when it played Chicago, which breaks my heart. I could not afford to go to the theatre in those days, beyond the 25-cent admission at the WPA theatres, so I never did see *Winterset*. But I read the play, fell in love with it, then saw the film, which I found very exciting although I didn't approve of all the cuts and the happy ending they tacked on. Something about the shape of the play, the way Maxwell Anderson used words, caught the fancy of a young theatre devotee, and I never have altered, although I haven't had many chances to work with it. When I was at Lafayette College in 1940, they produced it in the Little Theater, and I auditioned....

Friedman: You played in it.

Schaefer: ...and played your role of Esdras not very well, I fear, but I never was much of an actor. But at least I was around the play again. And then, I scheduled a production during those ten years that I was exclusively directing and producing the Hallmark Hall of Fame television shows. We did it live on a Sunday afternoon in a 90-minute version that played extremely well. The adaptation by Robert Hartung preserved both the spirit of the play and the flavor. The full play runs almost two and a half hours, uncut. A very nice cast: Don Murray played Mio, George C. Scott was Trock, Piper Laurie was Miriamne, and Marty Balsam was Garth. One of those typical all-star Hallmark casts, and I enjoyed directing it. Mrs. Anderson came to the final runthrough and was very pleased, and felt that Maxwell Anderson, had he still been with us, would have approved the production. I have a tape of it which I saw for the first time last year. It was picked up for delayed broadcast on the West Coast. Those were the days we would do shows live in New York; they would be taped in California, and played there three hours later. Two copies of this old two-inch tape existed at NBC in Los Angeles, without anyone knowing about them. The production rights were owned by NBC and my company, but they were given by NBC to the Hallmark Company who sponsored the show but didn't have any ownership rights. They had stored *Winterset* along with some other tapes in Kansas City, didn't know what to do with them, and finally presented the whole works to the Archives here at UCLA. Going through a list of acquisitions that the Archives have...there to my delight was *Winterset* on color tape. I had a cassette made so that I could study it, and see whether or not I wanted to spend the money and the time to preserve it because those old two-inch tapes are just on the verge of coming apart and I have decided that I will do that. It's not a perfect production, by any means, but it certainly is historically interesting, and there are so few versions of *Winterset* around....

Freidman: Now Anderson wrote, of course, other verse-plays... so what drew you to *Winterset*, as against, perhaps, some of his other verse-plays?

Schaefer: The fact that it is a modern gangster story, based on his strong convictions about the Sacco-Vanzetti case. He had written about the case in an earlier prose-play, *Gods of the Lightning*. But while his poetry seems appropriate in *Elizabeth the Queen* and *Mary of Scotland*, here it was unexpected. The same is true of *High Tor*, the play that followed this, a lighter, comedic play. Other plays of his that I like include *The Star Wagon*, a delightful prose-comedy with one or two poetic speeches attached. Not true, however, of *Wingless Victory*, which is a most interesting play, one that I would like to see again. Katherine Cornell played Princess Oparre in the original which was a wonderful evening in the theatre. When Bill Ward asked me what I would be interested in directing this year I had two or three suggestions, but *Winterset* was my favorite, and he said, "Well, for heaven's sake, do it".... *Winterset* represents a form of theater which seemed to be blossoming when I was in my late teens and twenties, and which has almost completely ceased to be. Maybe it will come again in years to come, but this material was utterly new to today's students. This was the time that Christopher Fry was writing, that Eliot and MacLeish were writing. There was a desire to write poetry for the theater—not as good poets, any of them, as Shakespeare, but in their own ways trying to use words in a way that the English language had been used earlier. At their best, I found them most exciting evenings in the theatre, and I really miss them. Today the plays are...grunts and groans, sprinkled with profanity, and occasionally a good plot. There have been exceptions. A lot of Tennessee Williams, even though he didn't write in a poetic form, is pure poetry, particularly *Glass Menagerie*. And a great deal of O'Neill was really poetry, written as prose. Today's playwrights, and I like a great many of them, will attempt the long soliloquy or the bold, big speech, but not in the way that Fry or Anderson or Eliot or Shakespeare wrote them.

Friedman: Of course, you've known that none of the students nor the present audience would probably be familiar with Anderson or this play. And that must have presented some kind of a problem to you, in terms of your expectations and your directorial approach.

Schaefer: Well, it was a challenge in terms of the students, which is what I liked. They are here to be educated, and knowing about plays like this and the problems of playing in them should be an essential part of their education. The fact that audiences are not used to hearing modern poetry worried me more. I had nightmares that half of the house would walk out in the first 20 minutes, saying, "People don't talk like that." But, I'm pleased to see they haven't. I think we lose a few at the intermission every night, but in general the audience...seems to stick with it....

Friedman: ...How are you able to read the audience?

Schaefer: Well, my usual criterion is head movement. I stand in the back of the auditorium on the side and watch heads. If the heads wiggle, I know we are losing them, but if they are glued to the stage, and you can hear a pin drop, you can be sure they are involved....

Friedman: What kind of a head-bob count have you had so far?

Schaefer: Well, we have been doing very well, very well. Even with that rather difficult Saturday night audience the first scene in the second act, particularly, had them absolutely engrossed.... There are a lot of very amusing lines, and twists and turns in the show, and I think audiences are a little shy about laughing

151

because they're not obvious. When Mio says, after he has spoken up for the policeman, "The only drawback is that being on the force infects the brain, eats the cerebrum," and a little ripple runs through the audience, you know they are hanging on every syllable. When Shadow comes in dripping and with all the deaths at the end, Anderson is stretching melodrama to its limits. There are always some people that get a little edgy in melodrama, but I think that we have held them very well.

Friedman: What kind of an approach do you feel that you, as George Schaefer, have made to this play that perhaps would be, or is different from another director?...

Schaefer: ...I think every director, particularly with a play as challenging as this, has his own approach. I did not try to superimpose either a style or a concept onto the material. I simply tried to dig into the material to get all the meanings, uncover all the relationships. I think we ended up with a very superior ground plan. Don Crabs, who designed the setting, came up with a scheme much superior, I think, to the ground plan on the original production. Of course, the soaring majesty of Mielziner's bridge, and the money to cover it with velour, were missed. The acting approach was to not shy away from the poetry, but to use it. At the very beginning, I had Trock move down center, look out over the heads of the audience, as though he was looking at the lights of Manhattan, and deliver the first speech as though it was a Shakespearean soliloquy. At the end of the play...we have Esdras go to almost the same position and deliver the beautiful valedictory, in the same way. When the purple passages came, particularly the ones that Mio has, I tried to stage things so that the positioning would be right.... Some of the problems that exist in our theatre forced my directional choices. We have a very, very wide auditorium, much too wide for the size of the theatre. It's wonderful backstage, but with a 40-foot proscenium opening, and with audiences spread out I guess, over 75 feet at least, I had to move the actors around the stage more....

Freidman: ...I wonder if you felt any kind of trepidation in approaching this play and trying to do it with young, untried performers in a university situation?

Schaefer: Yes, I certainly did, because it is about as difficult a play as one can find for any actors. Even in its original production in New York, to judge by the reviews, they had a lot of problems, particularly with Richard Bennett, who played the judge, and who apparently couldn't remember. Also with the actor... who played Esdras, who was mushy, and with those two roles hard to hear, the play must have been in certain difficulty.... Fortunately, Burgess Meredith and Margo and Ciannelli and others of the cast were so brilliant that it ran for quite a time and won those awards. At auditions, I insisted that everybody do some Shakespeare. I figured that would be a pretty good indication if they had some idea how to breathe and use words....

Freidman: ...Putting Maxwell Anderson together with young, mostly inexperienced, aspiring performers from college, did the cast provide any surprises for you, on either side of the ledger?

Schaefer: Well, let me see. [Pause] No, I wouldn't say so. They had some difficulties with the verse. We were very strict about being word-perfect and are somewhere in the 98 percents, I guess. I believe no matter what you are playing, the author's words are what you must interpret. I can't stand paraphrasing, which can be so contagious.... If the author's worth doing, it's worth doing the lines the way he wrote them. No, I don't think I could say that there were any unpleasant surprises. The most gratifying surprises were then, suddenly, a scene came to life that had not been, because of the difficulties with the verse, working particularly. In the case of [the actor playing Mio] he had delighted me, oh, at least five or six times in the course of the performances and the playing.... When you explain that at the end of that first scene of the second act, when you learn that your father's innocent, then after all the ecstasy and the excitement, you find that because of this girl you've let the cops go, and you're probably in the death-trap, a different dimension comes in; it's as though you are suddenly older than you were. But we'd already talked about the fact that he and Miriamne may be of an age but he's twice as old as she is in experience. You're an older man looking down on what's going on, and lines like "the bright ironical gods, what fun they have in heaven" are taken from a distance. If you play them as he was doing that [preview] night, as something a young man was experiencing in the room right then, it would never work. I said, "It may be dumb direction, but I've got to give it to you, because without it, it's nothing. Your whole attitude must change there." By God, the next night, he caught it exactly, and suddenly those difficult lines began to gel and fall into place.

Friedman: But I found him and all members of the cast, most receptive. I haven't seen any resistance.

Schaefer: No. That is true. I don't usually, I must honestly admit. Through these 244 professional directing jobs, I can count on the fingers of one hand the actors and actresses with whom I found it impossible to work, resisting, or stupid, or stubborn, or not liking what I was giving them. On *Winterset* I think they would have tried anything, really. At no point did anybody come out and say "I can't do that," or "that's a terrible idea." Sometimes we tried things that didn't work, and we'd go back and do it the way we had it yesterday. My directing style is to make the actor work, to make them feel before it's over that they've really done it all themselves. In a play like this, it's a little harder than in a realistic play, because you do have to superimpose a certain amount of—what shall I say—rhythm and poetry. But I don't think I ever said to anybody who came up with an idea that it wasn't worth trying. Sometimes they worked; sometimes they didn't. If they did work, we incorporated them. People tried things in rehearsals, and even in some of the early performances, and I would say, "that was a nice idea" or "that was dumb...." The thought of Shadow picking up Garth's violin and making him retrieve it just before he hears about the judge worked so well. It's just the sort of thing that would happen and was something they dreamed up themselves. Yet another piece of business the same two thought of was just terrible, and we knocked it out the first time we saw it....

Friedman: Now, I want to ask you about techniques again.... You got down to work right away. There was no talking, no sitting around a table and saying, "Let's open this up and analyze this, that and the next thing"....

Schaefer: ...That's a method I approve. A lot of directors don't. A lot of directors sit around for days, thinking and talking, and maybe they get better productions when it's all over, I don't know. I couldn't work that way. I find it best to have one reading, with a chance for questions. By reading that Rover Garland review of the original production to the cast, it gave them a sense of the importance I attach to the play, and I told them I was open to all questions of interpretation and interrelationships, but rather than sit around and probe and probe and probe, I just prefer to get the show on its feet. Two- thirds of the questions that come up are answered once you are on your feet, when you know what the set's like, where the other people are, and your relationship to them. By the time you have gone through the mechanics of movement, and have learned the words, then you are able to work on the other important things. Answers to so many questions just come out in the blocking and the memorization period. I never felt pressed for time, never said, "We can't talk about that; we've got to get on with it." As I said, I was doing a very straightforward production, taking the valuing from the script. If this had been a stylized version...you have different problems. But here it was just a case of digging into the words, digging into the characters, and thinking. I treated it as a realistic play, and with everything we tried to do, we tried to make sense.

Friedman: ...You certainly had a terrific reverence...for the Maxwell Anderson play, and in no way did you tamper with the text or the spirit of the play.

Schaefer: Well, I think a lot of that tampering goes on.... Charles Marowitz does his own productions of Shakespeare and Ibsen, with mixed results. Occasionally, they have been fascinating. Usually, they're disasters. I saw a sketch in a scenery book, I think it was from Yugoslavia, of *Winterset*. It was a bare platform, with a few twigs here and there. It was a unit set supposed to represent both the bridge and the room and it didn't look like either. But I'm sure the whole production was geared to this style. To do *Winterset* in commedia style for example, seems to me ludicrous, but maybe somebody could make it exciting. It's perfectly acceptable for a director to do that when everybody knows that's what the director is doing.... I think Beckett went too far last year with his objection to small scenic details. I regard the director as an interpreter. If you are going to write, you should write, and be an author, maybe be an author *and* a director. But if you are strictly a director, I think your function is to interpret the words of the author, and by "interpret," I mean bring them to life on stage so they communicate the author's message to an audience, and not use them to prove some theory of your own, or disprove some theory of your own. Great directors in that way (Tyrone Guthrie, to me, was the finest) are able to take a far out concept and make it work. Peter Brook did that quite brilliantly, I thought, with his *Dream* production. In England, they've done so much Shakespeare that when Stratford attacks *Winter's Tale* for the fourteenth time, they say, "What can we do with it, that we haven't done before?" They are pretty strict about sticking to the text even when they set the plays in different times. That wonderful production of *The Merchant of Venice* at the National with Olivier as Shylock, was set in subtle Jacobean browns in a completely different period than Shakespeare intended, but done with such consistency and brilliance that it seemed as though it had been written that way, and all the words were just the way they had been originally. The naughty ones are where, in order to fulfill a visual concept, directors twist the words, cut them out, change them, even take scenes from other plays, to make the scheme work. A perfect example of interpretation was the Orson Welles *Caesar* production at the Mercury Theater, where he imposed the fascistic uniforms and thinking into the play without changing a word and gave it tremendous impact. I don't direct that way. I have tried occasionally experimenting in style but, as a rule, I say I like these words, I like this music, I like what's here, and if it's not good enough to hold up on its own, I don't want to do it. In the film world you sometimes get a real piece of cheese and so much money to do it, that you say, "What can I do to make this bearable?" It's so much easier with film, because the camera and the editing can hide a multitude of sins. In the theater, you can't do that. The stage is there, and the audience is there, and you can only do so much hocus-pocus.

Friedman: ...Is there some question that you may have hoped that I would ask, or something that I have neglected to ask, that you think you would like to give an answer to? Have I missed something?

Schaefer: No, I don't think so. I treated *Winterset* as though I were directing it for Broadway or for the Ahmanson.... But it's a scary play for a commercial house that big. And perhaps with some justification. I think style-wise, it would fit beautifully in the Ahmanson, and there aren't many plays about which I can say that. Here at UCLA the financial risk is non- existent, the artistic risk is purely personal, and everybody is out to do the very best he can, to make audiences happy they came, and create a production you can look back on proudly. One final anecdote: When we were first auditioning, and I wasn't sure that he would get the part, I told [the actor playing Mio] that I admired his work in *Romeo and Juliet*...and so I hoped he would be auditioning for this. He said, "Well, I don't think I can because my agents get so mad at me." He had played Tybalt in *Romeo and Juliet* and missed out on a big movie there. "I think if I say that I am not available for another eight-ten weeks, whatever, that they'll just...." I gave him a good, strong lecture: "I've never heard anything so stupid. You're going to have your whole life to play these piddling parts in series and the films that you're being offered. I'm not sure that you are going to get it yet, but if you do, I guarantee it will be the only time in your life you will play Mio in *Winterset*, in a production with the size and the aspirations that we have for this one." So he went home and thought about it...and came back the next day, and said, "I told my agent to shove it. I'm going to do this if you want me."

Friedman: Thank you.

Maxwell Anderson in the 1980s:

An Annotated Bibliography

by William R. Klink,
Charles County Community College

The reputation that Maxwell Anderson earned in his lifetime has continued to develop long after his death. In the decade of the 1980s, scholars, friends, and people of the theater have continued to write of Anderson and his works almost in uniformly glowing terms. They have found his plays to contain nuances of meaning and art that in decades before had not been noticed. In addition to the new interpretations of Anderson's art, there has also been a broader movement to include Anderson in the pantheon of the greatest American dramatists by giving him extensive space in the standard reference books on American drama. A review of the bibliography of material on Anderson reveals, then, two separate but noteworthy trends, reinterpretation and canonization.

Among the reinterpreters, critics who happen to be women, who read Anderson perhaps from a different point of view than earlier scholars, who were almost uniformly male, have made some of the most important observations. Kathleen Trainer's *The Dissident Character in American Drama of the 1930s* (1983) studies Anderson as a conservative during that period. Helen Chinoy and Linda Jenkins in *Women in American Theatre* (1987, expanded from the original 1981 volume) give an interesting view of Bus in *Both Your Houses*. Both have produced work that reveals a side of Anderson's dramaturgy that previously had either been undervalued or overlooked. Their views provide a complement to those expressed by Alfred Shivers, who produced in the 1980s two important books on Anderson, the superb *The Life of Maxwell Anderson* in 1983 and *Maxwell Anderson: An Annotated Bibliography of Primary and Secondary Works* in 1985.

On the other hand, much of the writing on Anderson in this decade has appeared in encyclopedias and reference books, such as *Oxford Companion to American Literature*. While these are all short pieces, and, because of the purposes of the volumes in which they appear, necessarily superficial, the sheer numbers of such listings in this decade make Anderson one of the few playwrights in American theatrical history who will always be seen, known, and revered as one of the great ones.

For this bibliography which I have chosen to arrange by year so that readers may see the growth of the Anderson bibliography over time, I have scoured numerous libraries, indexes, and followed hunches. I have discovered inexact references in *The New York Times* index and book indexes which are inaccurate. Recognizing that compiling an annotated bibliography is a Sisyphean task, even in the age of computers, I would not be surprised if there are references still to be found which might augment this list. Fortunately, there will always be the opportunity for updates, as Anderson undoubtedly will continue to occupy a place of inquiry for those interested in the American theater.

Other Work by Anderson

1987

The Masque of Queens. Hinsdale, New York: Anderson House.

Works on Anderson

1980

Bronner, Edward. *The Encyclopedia of the American Theatre 1900-1975.* New York: A. S. Barnes.
> There are many brief citations of Anderson's plays throughout the volume. Plays are listed by title.

Bergman, Ingrid, and Alan Burgess. *Ingrid Bergman [:] My Story.* New York: Delacorte.
> Says Anderson personally called Bergman to do *Joan of Lorraine* and tells how she relented on the beach in Santa Monica. Chapter II tells of her version of events of the play itself, how she got Anderson to change the play, how she was afraid of the moviescript's lacking quality (169-84).

Corry, John. "Stage: Estelle Parsons in 'Elizabeth and Essex.'" *The New York Times*, February 25, C 15:1.
> Corry calls the new musical at the South Street Theater "fascinating." He says that *Elizabeth the Queen* on which it is based is a "neglected play, fallen from favor because it is not much about passion as it is about suppressed passion."

Garfield, David. *A Player's Place [:] The Story of the Actor's Studio.* New York: Macmillan.
Very little about Anderson here, except to note Anderson's dislike of the talkativeness of Strasberg and Clurman.

Luckett, Perry D. "*Winterset* and Some Early Eliot Poems." *North Dakota Quarterly*, 48 (Summer), 26-37.
Luckett looks at the relationship between the play and Eliot's major poems. His conclusion is that Eliot is as important to Anderson as Shakespeare was.

Mason, Jeffrey D. "Maxwell Anderson's Dramatic Theory and *Key Largo*." *North Dakota Quarterly*, 48 (Summer), 38-52.
Mason argues that Anderson married theory and practice, intending "his verse to *serve* theme, character, and structure, instead of taking precedence over them" (30), his role to affirm the human spirit. Mason's analysis of *Key Largo*, using the theories he says were Anderson's, leads to a clear understanding of Anderson's sometimes difficult-to-understand methodologies.

Orlin, Lena Cowen. "*Night Over Taos*: Maxwell Anderson's Sources and Artistry." *North Dakota Quarterly*, 48 (Summer), 12-25.
Orlin in a painstaking manner establishes that *American Mercury* articles by Harvey Fergusson and Racine's *Mithridates* are sources for the play.

Palmieri, Anthony F. R. *Elmer Rice: A Playwright's Vision of America.* Rutherford, NJ: Fairleigh Dickinson UP.
Palmieri gives a brief synopsis of the founding of the Playwright's Company by Anderson and the others. An interesting note to *Street Scene* tells of how William H. Brody, that play's original producer, allowed Rice to select a director. Rice chose George Cukor, who then abandoned the project for Anderson's *Gypsy* (95). Palmieri thinks Rice the equal of Anderson (196). Some of the index citations are incorrect in this volume.

Sahu, N. S. "*Winterset*: A Tragedy by a Gifted Technician." *Commonwealth Quarterly*, 4 (March), 3-15.
Sahu argues that the play uses Shakespeare as a source, and that additionally its imagery is drawn from science and technology. It is not melodrama, in Sahu's view, but rather a very successful play.

Sanders, Ronald. *The Days Grow Short: A Life and Music of Kurt Weill*. New York: Holt.
Sanders says Weill needed Anderson's friendship to be creative, including helping him find a house near Anderson's as well as the collaborations for the theatre. Weill's dependence on Anderson seems to extend to Weill's collaborations with others, such as Rice in *Street Scene*, which Anderson apparently abetted (349). Sanders gives quite a bit of space to *Lost in the Stars* (375-388, 391-92) and *Knickerbocker Holiday* (269- 82), in addition to the *Huckleberry Finn* project (396).

Smeall, J. F. S. "Additions to the Maxwell Anderson Bibliography." *North Dakota Quarterly*, 48 (Summer), 60- 63.
Smeall adds 23 items to the previously compiled list by Laurence Avery. All are college pieces done by Anderson at the University of North Dakota.

Smock, Susan Wanless. "*Lost in the Stars* and *Cry, the Beloved Country*: A Thematic Comparison." *North Dakota Quarterly*, 48 (Summer), 53-59.
Smock argues that Anderson's story is stronger, less tentative than Paton's and as a result is more hopeful.

Tees, Arthur T. "Maxwell Anderson's Changing Attitude Toward War." *North Dakota Quarterly*, 48 (Summer), 5-11.
Tees argues that Anderson over the years moved from the anti-war position of *What Price Glory* to arguing in favor of nuclear war against Russia in an article for *The New York Times*. Tees says the change was caused by Anderson's growing recognition of the "validity of the struggle between good and evil." He saw democracy as a good force worth fighting for.

1981

Anon. *The National Cyclopedia of American Biography*. Clifton, NJ: James T. White, 323-25.
The writer gives a multi-page biography of Anderson centering it on his plays and their performances.

Avery, Laurence G. "Maxwell Anderson." *Dictionary of Literary Biography, Vol. 7: Twentieth Century American Dramatists*, Part 1, A-J. Ed. John MacNicholas. Detroit: Gale, 23-35.

Avery discusses Anderson's work briefly, focusing on *What Price Glory* and Anderson's other great plays.

Brenman-Gibson, Margaret. *Clifford Odets: American Playwright.* New York: Atheneum.
Brenman-Gibson gives some interesting if passing references to the intersection of Anderson's career with that of Odets.

Leonard, William Torbert, ed. *Theatre: Stage to Screen to Television.* Vol. 1. Metuchen, NJ: Scarecrow, 2 vols., *passim.*
References to Anderson include those to *Elizabeth the Queen, Key Largo, Mary of Scotland, The Masque of Kings, Saturday's Children, Winterset, Knickerbocker Holiday,* and Anderson's screen adaptation of *A Christmas Carol.*

Mordden, Ethan. *The American Theatre.* New York: Oxford UP.
Mordden says that *What Price Glory* was a not understood platonic homosexual sublimation piece (107), and *Gods of the Lightning* is the best early example of an American political play (121). He discusses the "odd naturalism"of *Winterset* as part of Anderson's working out of his own moral system one play at a time (151-59). Many other passing references.

Ward, A. C. and Maurice Hussey. *Longman Companion to Twentieth Century Literature,* 3rd ed. Burnt Hills, Harlow, England: Longman.
A brief biographical sketch, although longer than the one provided Sherwood Anderson but shorter in length than the entry for *Androcles and the Lion* in the same volume (18).

1982

Anon. "Maxwell Anderson," *Academic American Encyclopedia.* Danbury, CT: Grolier, Vol. 1, 402.
A brief biography.

Anon. "Maxwell Anderson (1888-1959),"*Encyclopedia International.* Fairfax, VA: Lexicon, Vol. 1, 389-90.
A brief biography.

Brockett, Oscar. *Modern Theatre: Realism and Nationalism to the Present.* Boston: Allyn, 93, 97-99, 119.

Repeats material cited in earlier and later volumes, comparing Anderson to O'Neill as American's greatest dramatists.

Gassner, John. "The Possibilities and Perils of Modern Tragedy." *Tragedy [:] Vision and Form*, 2nd ed. New York: Harper, 304.
Article originally published in the *Tulane Drama Review* in 1957.

Harris, Richard H. *Modern Drama in England and America 1950- 1970*. Detroit: Gale, 66-67.
Bibliography.

Jarman, Douglas. *Kurt Weill: An Illustrated Biography*. Bloomington: Indiana UP, *passim*.
Jarman gives details of the first Anderson-Weill collaboration, *Knickerbocker Holiday*. Jarman mentions *Ulysses Africanus*, a play abandoned by the team, and the cantata *Magna Carta* of 1940, and finally *Lost in the Stars* of 1949. Jarman points out that *Huckleberry Finn* was uncompleted by the two only because of Weill's death.

Klink, William R. "Maxwell Anderson and S. N. Behrman: A Reference Guide Updated." *Resources for American Literary Study*, 12 (Autumn), 195-214.
This annotated bibliography updates Klink's *Maxwell Anderson and S. N. Behrman: A Reference Guide* of 1977. Despite the 1982 publication date, material cited extends in one case to 1983. The bulk of the listings terminate, however, in 1980. The present bibliography is an update of the *RALS* study.

Langer, Elinor. *Josephine Herbst*. New York: Little Brown.
Langer discusses Herbst's meeting the husband of her friend Margaret Anderson, the future playwright Maxwell, in February 1920. Then Langer details how Maxwell Anderson pursued Herbst romantically thereafter, claiming Anderson "deflowered" Herbst, and telling of his lingering attachment to Margaret (55- 58). The affair was over by the summer of 1920. It is implied that Anderson gave Herbst money in exchange for their letters and then destroyed them (78-79). Langer makes Anderson's not paying for the abortion of his and Herbst's child seem to be the action of a lout (60).

1983

Clurman, Harold. *The Fervent Years.* New York: DaCapo.
Clurman, in this edition of the book, says that Anderson was eager to join the Group Threater, engaging in friendly artistic arguments. Later arguments, however, extended to the language of Anderson's plays, particularly *Night Over Taos*, which Clurman was reluctant to let the Group Theatre do. Clurman goes on to say that the play was financed by Franchot Tone, Anderson, and Dorothy Patten's father (76-81).

Hart, James D., ed. *Oxford Companion to American Literature*, 5th ed. New York: Oxford UP, *passim*.
The volume gives brief articles on Anderson and some of his plays.

Hartnoll, Phyllis. *The Oxford Companion to the Theatre*, 4th ed. New York: Oxford UP.
This volume contains only a brief article on Anderson (26-27).

Leonard, William T. *Broadway Bound: A Guide to Shows.* Metuchen, NJ: Scarecrow.
Anderson is cited only for *Dark Victory* in a book about plays that did not make Broadway. This play died in New Haven Dec. 30, 1953. Leonard gives some reviews and updates to its becoming *Stolen Hours* in the 1963 film version starring Susan Hayward (116-117).

Loney, Glenn. *Twentieth Century Theatre.* New York: Facts on File Publications, *passim*.
Done by year and country, this volume includes brief snippets on Anderson's plays until 1947.

Luckett, Perry. "Maxwell Anderson." *The Encyclopedia of the United States of America.* Ed. R. Alton Lee. Gulf Breeze, FL: American International Press, Vol. 3.
Luckett gives a brief description of Anderson's career and a bibliography of works on Anderson (31-32).

Shivers, Alfred S. *The Life of Maxwell Anderson.* Briarcliff Manor, New York: Stein.

By far the best piece on Anderson, this biography makes full use of Shivers' long-time study of Anderson. It provides the names, the dates, and the ambiance of Anderson's public and private sides. Included is a striking set of old photographs of Anderson, his associates, and the places of their activities. This volume is painstakingly researched and proudly rendered.

Trainer, Kathleen Malise. *The Dissident Character in American Drama of the 1930s*, Ph.D. Diss. U of Notre Dame.
Trainer looks at the 14 dramas Anderson produced during the 1930s, citing him as the only conservative among a group including himself, Behrman, Lawson, Rice, and Odets. Trainer says that the dissident characters in the dramas were used to express the dramatist's political views, as well as the dramatist's characteristics—intelligence, resourcefulness, articulateness, sensitivity, and broad reading. They act out of idealism to improve society. Anderson's plays use that character as a hero, placing him in an historical era in which an old order is challenged by a new one. Trainer points out that Anderson's characters stand out above others in the plays because they are presented as being morally superior. With the exception of the one-act dramas, the dissident character is the protagonist of the play; he is introduced in the first act and embroiled in complications that make him doubt his motive in the second act. Finally, in the last act, he redeems himself as the old order reasserts itself, and he becomes heroic. Chapter I, "The Dissident Character As the Hero," is devoted to Anderson.

1984

Bordman, Gerald. *The Oxford Companion to American Theatre*. New York: Oxford UP.
The volume gives a brief biography of Anderson, citing Shivers' biography (27-28). Also cited are dates, casts, synopses, and reviews of *What Price Glory, Saturday's Children, Gypsy, Elizabeth the Queen, Both Your Houses, Mary of Scotland, Valley Forge, Winterset, Wingless Victory, High Tor, The Star Wagon, Knickerbocker Holiday, Key Largo, Anne of the Thousand Days, Lost in the Stars,* and important people with whom Anderson's career was entwined.

Dasgupta, Gautam. "Anderson, Maxwell." *McGraw-Hill Encyclopedia of World Drama*. Ed. Stanley Hochman et, al, 2nd ed. New York: McGraw-Hill. Vol. 1.
  The Anderson entry is quite extensive (137-143) and complemented by illustrations.

Klein, Alvin. "Stamford Celebrates the Plays of Maxwell Anderson." *The New York Times*, September 30, 23, 24:1.
  Klein reports that on the twenty-fifth anniversary of Anderson's death the premiere of one of his unpublished plays, *The Masque of Queens*, at the Ethel Kweskin Barn Theater in Stamford, Connecticut, accompanies the films of *Key Largo* and *Elizabeth and Essex*. He gives a brief history of the celebration started in 1982.

Salem, James M. *A Guide to Critical Reviews, Part I American Drama 1909-1982*. 3rd ed. Metuchen, NJ: Scarecrow.
  Salem gives an extensive listing of the reviews of Anderson's plays as well as their opening date and the number of performances (19-31). This is an impressive compilation.

1985

Atkinson, Brooks. *Broadway*. New York: Limelight.
  In this edition, an update of the 1970 volume, Atkinson mentions Anderson in context of the Theatre Guild. The winners of the New York Drama Critics Circle Award of 1936 are pictured with Anderson among them for *Winterset* (254). There is also the story of its awarding (262-265). Then Atkinson gives a history of the development of the Playwright's Company in a chapter called "The Big Five." Atkinson says Helen Hayes moved from popular star to serious actress in Anderson's *Mary of Scotland* (337). There are other passing citations as well.

Bloom, Harold. ed. *Twentieth Century American Literature, Vol. 1*. New York: Chelsea.
  The material on Maxwell Anderson (175-180) includes pieces by Edmund Wilson and a reprint of Edward Foster's "Care of Belief: An Interpretation of the Plays of Maxwell Anderson" from *SWR*, Winter 1942, 87-88.

Flanagan, Hallie. *Arena: The Story of the Federal Theatre*. New York: Limelight.
> Flanagan writes of how Anderson was considered a "dangerous author"for a performance of *Valley Forge* (225). She reveals that Anderson got $10 or so as royalty for every performance of his plays by the Federal Theatre Project (263). This book, the story of the project from the point of view of its Director, adds to knowledge of the era as a whole and of Anderson in particular.

Klein, Alvin. "Anderson Play in Stamford Series." *The New York Times*, October 6, 26, 28:5.
> Klein calls *Sea-wife* "a mood piece that is rife with symbolism." It was performed as part of the Maxwell Anderson Playwright Series of the Stamford Community Arts Council.

Levine, Ira. *Left-Wing Dramatic Thinking in American Theatre*. Ann Arbor: UMI Research Press.
> Levine gives a brief list of some of Anderson's plays as a footnote in Chapter II, "Incipient Left-Wing Dramatic Theory in the 1920s" in a section called "Realism Reemerges." After a lengthy discussion of *Gods of the Lightning* (69-77), Levine concludes that discussion with the statement, "The play had demonstrated that realism was a viable revolutionary form—still the means of inculcating a radical message and instilling radical fever"(77).

Shivers, Alfred S. *Maxwell Anderson: An Annotated Bibliography of Primary and Secondary Works*. Metuchen, NJ: Scarecrow.
> Shivers' work is a masterful compilation of Anderson's writings, published and unpublished, secondary sources (written and oral), and a listing of master's theses. It took Shivers over a decade to amass this quantity of information. The useful material ends about 1983. Despite the title, only a small percentage of the items are annotated. The book is arranged in sections, containing Anderson's writings, "Primary Works," and "Secondary Works." The listing in "Secondary Works" of "Book Length Studies of Anderson," then "Shorter Items of a General Nature about Anderson or His Work," then "Reviews and Other Writings About the Longer Works," then "Doctoral Dissertations and Master's Theses," then "Bibliographies and Check-Lists," and finally "Recorded Interviews Conducted by Alfred Shivers" all

presuppose that the researcher already knows what the item
is that he is researching, a limitation of listing by type rather
in another way.

1986

Gussow, Mel. "Theater: Weill's 'Lost in the Stars' at Long Wharf." *The New
York Times*, April 30, C 26:1.
Gussow says that Anderson took a "simplistic view" of
South Africa and of Paton's novel.

Henderson, Mary C. *The Theater in America*. New York: Abrams.
Contains a brief mention of Anderson and the Theatre Guild
(333).

Lappin, Louis. "Lost in the Stars by Maxwell Anderson and Kurt Weill. Long
Wharf Theatre, New Haven, Conn., 22 May 1986." *Theatre Journal*
38 (4 December), 479-80.
Lappin calls Arvin Brown's revival "theatrically compelling
and artfully conceived," but says it is no longer convincing
as a musical tragedy given current events in South Africa.

Leonard, William T. *Masquerade in Black*. Metuchen, NJ: Scarecrow.
This book about whites in blackface contains only two
passing references to Anderson. Helen Hayes is cited as
seeming physically larger in *Mary of Scotland* in a manner
similar to Kean in *Othello* (36).

Leonard, William T. *Once Was Enough*. Metuchen, NJ: Scarecrow.
In this volume, Leonard calls *The Bad Seed* "absorb-
ing"(32).

Staff of the Fenwick Library, George Mason University. *The Federal Theatre
Project: A Catalog-Calendar of Productions*. New York: Greenwood.
There are 13 references for Anderson listed in the Name Index of this
volume (232). *Saturday's Children*, listed six times, has half of the
listings for Anderson's plays which were done by the Federal Theatre
Project. These 12 productions are each separately described with the
citing of performance, the date of first performance, the theatre, and
references to the classification of each artifact held by the Fenwick
Library in the Production Catalog section.

1987

Adler, Thomas P. *Mirror on the Stage: The Pulitzer Plays as an Approach to American Drama*. W. Lafayette, IN: Purdue UP.
Both Your Houses was the only Anderson play which won a Pulitzer. Adler discusses it in the context of what its selection shows about the theatre of its time.

Brockett, Oscar G. *History of the Theatre*. 5th ed. Boston: Allyn.
Brockett briefly describes Anderson's work, ranking him with O'Neill. This is the same material as in previous volumes of Brockett's (633-655).

Chinoy, Helen K., and Linda W. Jenkins. *Women in American Theatre*. New York: Crown (revised and expanded from the 1981 edition).
In a section on the images of female characters, Chinoy and Jenkins say that Bus in *Both Your Houses* is the only character in this study without involvement in a love story in plays from 1918-39 (247). Bus, as a secretary, is in the middle ground of working women studied in plays of the time period.

Magill, Frank. *Critical Survey of Drama, Vol. 1*. Englewood Cliffs: Salem.
The Anderson citation (24-25) hits the highlights of Anderson's career and includes a short bibliography.

Murphy, Brenda. *American Realism and American Drama 1880-1940*. New York: Cambridge UP.
After noting that Anderson followed Sherwood's *The Road to Rome* with his own *Both Your Houses* in the genre of serious plays about patriotism and war (169), Murphy points out in an extended passage how *Saturday's Children* "brings the conventional romantic dream of a happy-ever-after ending up against the postwar reality of inadequate salaries, high prices, and scarce, expensive housing"(180). She remarks on *What Price Glory* (170-71) that it is a play which "exchanged one set of romantic ideals for another"in its characterization of Quirt and Flagg despite its "realistic deflation of the glory of war." The book is a study of literary realism as it evolved in American drama. The remarks are in the last chapter, "The Final Integration: Innovation in Realistic Thought and Structure"(1916-40).

Klein, Alvin. "Readings Series Broadens Its Scope." *The New York Times*,
October 18, 23, 35:1.
Klein comments on the fifth year of the Maxwell Anderson
Playwrights Series, which for the first time did not open with
an Anderson play. Gilda Anderson is quoted as saying that
the unproduced *Madonna and Child* should be done.

1988

Anon. *Maxwell Anderson and the Playwright's Producing Company*. New
York: The Historical Society of Rockland County.
This is a catalog which accompanied the exhibition at The
New York Public Library at Lincoln Center of artifacts of
Anderson's career in conjunction with the 1988-89 celebra-
tion of Anderson's birth. The material on the Playwright's
Producing Company by Dorothy L. Swerdlove is aug-
mented by some fine photographs.

Arthur, Kay. *A Guide to the Films of Maxwell Anderson*. Stamford, CT: The
Ferguson Library.
Arthur details all the films that have been made from the
plays of Anderson, including a brief summary, the stars, the
directors, the studios, the dates, the length, whether in color
or black and white. She also provides the same information
for the original screenplays of Anderson. An interesting
facet is the summaries of screenplays to which Anderson
contributed. The pamphlet was produced in conjunction
with the Maxwell Anderson Centennial Celebration.

Goodman, Walter. "Exploring the Turmoil of South Africa." *The New York
Times*, March 31, C 21, 1.
Goodman says that now *Lost in the Stars* ends "like a liberal
pipe dream," in a production at the York Theater.

Afterword:

Maxwell Who?

by Alan H. Anderson,
New City, New York

The response to the event of my father's Centennial[1] celebration has been extremely gratifying to all his admirers, his family among them. The various efforts on his behalf have been going on for almost three years and this volume of essays is a very fitting and appropriate coda. The participants in the rite have appeared from all over the country and have counted among their number theatre people, scholars, educators, journalists, friends in public office and many others who could best be identified simply as audience.

One unanswered question, which arose with our first discussions of the celebration, still goes largely unanswered or produces several answers, none of which seems wholly satisfactory. The question is, why is Anderson not better known today, read more, studied more, and seen more often in production? Considering his prominence, critical acclaim, and popular success among theatre audiences over a period of 30 years, it seems puzzling.

Consider for moment some of the measures of his career as an American playwright:

He began with a self-imposed handicap by waiting until 1923 when he was 35 years old before writing his first commercially produced play. By contrast, John Keats, Dad's favorite poet, died at 34. With that relatively late start, Dad had written 35 plays by the time of his death at age 70, 33 of which were produced before he died. That was an average of one play a year for the last 35 years of his life. During those same years, he wrote 11 Hollywood films, several radio plays, a book of verse, two books of essays on the theatre, and myriad published poems and articles.

Of the 36 produced plays, 27 were on Broadway, *Both Your Houses* won him a Pulitzer Prize in 1933, and the first two awards of the Drama Critics'

171

Circle for best play of the year went to *Winterset* for the 1935-36 season and to *High Tor* a season later.

At least 21 of his plays were box office successes and 19 of them were chosen for Burns Mantle's *Best Plays of the Year* volumes.

By comparison with two of his prolific contemporaries, Maxwell Anderson wrote two more plays than George Kaufman and seven more than his most formidable contemporary, Eugene O'Neill. And while O'Neill's plays were highly visible through the 1920s when Maxwell was just getting started, O'Neill was in almost total eclipse through the 30s and 40s when Anderson was represented on Broadway every year by at least one play and sometimes by two or even three.

Despite that history, as we mark the 100th anniversary of Anderson's birth, we find few of his plays in revival, even the best known of them are hard to find in print, and it is the rare high school senior who has ever heard of him.

In his review of Alfred Shivers' biography, *The Life of Maxwell Anderson*, Joshua Logan, the director,[2] asked, "...were his themes too sober? Was his style too conservative? Why is Eugene O'Neill revived and not Anderson? Why do we who bought theatre tickets through the 1920s and 1930s and 1940s know and revere him, while the equally passionate playgoers of today say,'Maxwell who?'"

Several possible reasons have been offered for Anderson's obscurity today: his themes are predominantly concerned with intellectual rather than emotional problems; his plays are expensive and difficult to produce because many of his casts are large and most of his plays require several sets; his themes are concerned with political or social problems of the particular time and are therefore "dated."

It is also suggested that the trouble might lie in Dad's preoccupation with language and specifically, his desire to write his plays in verse. He believed verse was the language of real tragedy, and many of his plays, not just historical, but modern, were in verse. Bear in mind, up to that point, poetry had been to him the ultimate form of language. He had been writing poetry since high school, had many published poems and had been one of the founders of *The Measure*, a prestigious poetry magazine.

When he wrote plays, his dialogue was often larger than life. Whereas we have had a love affair in this country with realism— with words that reflect the mundane—Maxwell Anderson wrote dialogue that swooped and soared, and carried us upward with the imagery and grandeur that only poetry can reach. Perhaps there is less hunger among today's theatre audiences for language that challenges our imaginative powers.

Perhaps he is less popular today because he would not settle for everyday language. One the other hand, many of his staunch admirers single out language as one of their reasons for their continuing interest in his work.

Is he less popular because he was not content to write about everyday people in everyday situations?

In October 1923, very early in his playwriting career, in a letter to Heywood Broun, Dad discussed his theories about what characters and what themes are worthy of a play:

> A great play cannot deal with ordinary people speaking commonplaces. It cannot deal with ordinary life. It has to concern itself with definitely unusual individuals in unusual situations, lifted by extraordinary emotions to extraordinary actions. And if it is to have the depth and reach of tragedy, it must pass before a setting that has in it something mysterious and titanic. It must rise above the usages of law, custom and religion into an elemental, spacious and timeless world, which we have all glimpsed but will never inhabit.

These would seem heavy demands coming from a novice playwright unless we remember that he tended to measure all playwriting—if not all writing—against the best of Shakespeare.

Fifteen years later, in 1938, when Dad had written several hits and by his own admission, several more failures, he attempted to formulate more specific theories on playwriting. It resulted in a volume of essays called *The Essence of Tragedy*[3], and in the title essay, he explained his struggle to understand what was characteristic of plays that became successes and what was lacking in the failures. Although the essay did not reaffirm the statement to Broun made in 1923, it became a guide to many professional writers and directors in the theater, including Joshua Logan and Burgess Meredith.

He gives us a sense of what is demanded of a hero with the following:

> The hero who is to make the central discovery in a play must not be a perfect man. He must have some variation of what Aristotle calls a tragic fault; and the reason he must have it is that when he makes the discovery, he must change both in himself and in his action—and he must change for the better—it is necessary that he must become more admirable, and not less so, at the end of the play.

And later Dad develops further this point of the "worth" or admirable qualities of the hero. He says we sometimes follow Sophocles "whose tragedy is always an exaltation of the human spirit, sometimes Euripedes, whose tragicomdey follows the same pattern of an excellence achieved through suffering." It seems clear that Dad felt the hero of a play should aspire to something higher, nobler.

The essay "The Essence of Tragedy" ends with these words:

> The theater at its best is a religious affirmation, an age-old rite restating and reassuring man's belief in his own destiny

173

and his ultimate hope. The theater is much older than the
doctrine of evolution, but its one faith, asseverated again and
again for every age and every year, is a faith in evolution,
in the reaching and the climb of men toward distant goals,
glimpsed but never seen, perhaps never achieved, or
achieved only to be passed impatiently on the way to a more
distant horizon.

Something of his hopes for the human race can be found in his essay called
"Whatever Hope We Have"[4] in which he suggests how we might evaluate our
writing, our lives and our arts:

"The test of a message is its continuing effect on the minds of men
over a period of generations."

"The nobler a man's interests the better citizen he is."

"If we are to be remembered as more than a mass of people who lived
and fought wars and died, it is for our arts that we will be remembered."

Perhaps if these determinations are reflected in his themes and his
heroes, there is something about his demand on us to be looking higher, to be
seeking excellence, which has had trouble finding audiences lately.

It may be that any or all of these reasons have some part in keeping
Maxwell Anderson from greater popularity today. But certainly the great
interest that has been shown in his work by those involved in every aspect of
the Centennial Celebration makes one hope that Anderson will continue to be
discovered and rediscovered in the years to come. This volume of essays on
his work does much to rekindle interest in his work and for that I am most
grateful.

Notes

1. Maxwell Anderson was born on December 15, 1888 in Atlantic, Pennsylvania.

2. Logan, one of Broadway's most successful directors from the late 30s to the 60s, was a great admirer of Anderson and director of his musical satire, *Knickerbocker Holiday*.

3. *The Essence of Tragedy and Other Footnotes and Papers*, Washington, DC: Anderson House, 1939.

4. In *The Essence of Tragedy*.

Index

F

Feast of Ortolans, 123
Fiddler on the Roof, 101
*First Flight,*74, 84, 87, 90
Frankfurter Zeitung und Handelsblatt, 116

G

Garson, Barbara, 54
Germania, 116
Gershwin, George, 54
Gershwin, Ira, 54
Ghosts, 119
Glengarry Glenn Ross, 55
Gods of the Lightning, 34, 72, 77, 84, 119
The Golden Six, 72
The Good Soldier Schweik, 115
Green, Paul, 28
Group Theater, 27, 34
Guild Board, 27
Gypsy, 72, 77

H

H.M.S.Pinafore, 101
Halline, Allen G., 60
Herald Tribune, 121
Hickerson, Harold, 28
High Tor, 3, 38, 121
Hopkins, Arthur, 10
Howard, Sidney, 12
Huckleberry Finn, 54

I

J

K

L

M

R

S